DISCARD

MYTHS OF THE WORLD

LEGENDS OF AFRICA

MYTHS OF THE WORLD

LEGENDS OF AFRICA

MWIZENGE TEMBO

MetroBooks

MetroBooks

AN IMPRINT OF FRIEDMAN/FAIRFAX PUBLISHERS

© 1999 by Michael Friedman Publishing Group, Inc.

All rights reserved. No part of this publication may be re-produced, stored in a retrieval system, or transmitted, in any form or by any means, electronic, mechanical, photo-copying, recording, or otherwise, without prior written permission from the publisher.

Library of Congress Cataloging-in-Publication data available upon request.

ISBN 1-56799-352-4

Editor: Stephen Slaybaugh
Art Director: Lynne Yeamans
Designer: Susan Livingston
Layout: Jonathan Gaines
Photography Editor: Deborah Bernhardt

Color separations by HBM Print Ltd.
Printed in China by Leefung-Asco Printers Ltd.

For bulk purchases and special sales, please contact:
Friedman/Fairfax Publishers
Attention: Sales Department
15 West 26th Street
New York, NY 10010
212/685-6610 FAX 212/685-1307

Visit our Website:
http://www.metrobooks.com

PHOTOGRAPHY CREDITS

© Art Resource, NY: Werner Forman Archive/British Museum, London: 67 top; Werner Forman Archive/Private Collection, London: 28

© Craig Brandt: 29

© Robin Brandt: 6

Courtesy of Dover Publications: 53, 75 left

© Dean Fox/Superstock: 30

FPG: © David Bartruff: 2, 63; © M. Corsetti: 12, 69; © Rob Gage: 34; © M.P. Kahl: 32, 33; © Stan Osolinski: 67 bottom; © Peter Tevis: 52–53

Jason Lauré Studios: © Jason Lauré: 13, 14, 18, 24–25, 26, 41, 47, 51, 56, 58–59, 70, 72–73, 78 right, 79, 81, 86, 88–89, 92, 93

Leo de Wys: © J. Boutin: 85; © D. Briscoe: 57; © Howard Gross: 73; © R. Nolan: 74

The National Museum of African Art, Smithsonian Institution: Photography by Eliot Elisofon, 1971, Eliot Elisofon Photographic Archives: 66 bottom; Photography by Franko Khoury, Museum purchase, 84-6-10: 16–17

© The Nelson-Atkins Museum of Art, Kansas City, MO (Purchase: Nelson Trust): 66 top

© Boyd Norton: 38 right, 90

© Dorian R. Romer: 27, 40, 48–49, 76

© SuperStock: British Museum, London: 64; Christie's, London: 16, 39, 61, 77; National Museum, Lagos, Nigeria/D. Forbert: 50

© Mwizenge Tembo: 55, 82 left

© Aldo Tutino/Art Resource: 19

© Richard Todd: Block Collection: 68 right; Hammer Collection: 35; Kuhn Collection: 10, 38 left, 54, 60, 75 right; Private Collection: 15, 22, 44; Stanoff Collection: 20; The Walt Disney-Tishman African Art Collection: 78 left

The Wildlife Collection: © Tim Laman: 62, 71

Woodfin Camp & Associates: © Marc and Evelyne Bernheim: 36–37, 42, 45, 46, 68 left, 80, 87, 88; © Betty Press: 23, 83, 84; Amos U. Schliack: 43

Map Art: © Emilya Naymark: 8

DEDICATION

I would like to dedicate this book to the memory of my grandparents, Mateyo Kabinda, Esitele Nya Mwaza, and Vayeya Mayovu; and also to Zibalwe Tembo.

ACKNOWLEDGMENTS

The folktales in this book were taken from the Tumbuka people, which is a Bantu tribe located in the Lundazi district of Eastern Zambia. They were recorded during two separate research field trips I took in April 1985 and August 1993. I am especially grateful for the assistance of the late Dominique Muchimba of the Institute of African Studies of the University of Zambia in recording these tales. In addition, the Office of the District Governor of the Lundazi district gave the research team invaluable help and hospitality. I would also like to thank the Institute of African Studies of the University of Zambia for sponsoring both of the field trips, and the Flory Faculty Development Fund of the Bridgewater College in Virginia, from which partial funding for the August 1993 field trip was obtained.

I would like to thank the men, women, and especially the children of Chimwala Village in Chief Mwase and Chimwamtaba Village in Chief Magodi in the Lundazi district for their enthusiasm and willingness to tell the folktales that I recorded, transcribed, and translated.

My gratitude goes to the following people for the animal legends they told me: my parents, Sani Zibalwe Tembo and Enelesi Nya Kabinda, and the late Tirabirenji Tembo of Zibalwe Village in the Lundazi district of Eastern Zambia, Smart Nyoni of Mtema Village, my grandparents the late Mateyo Kabinda and Esitele Nya Mwaza of Chipewa Village, Joseph John Mayovu and Dikilani Mayovu of Seleta Village, and Noah Tonga of Chief Chikomeni. (In the Tumbuka language of the Lundazi district of Eastern Zambia, the prefix *Nya* is normally inserted before a young or adult woman's last name as a sign of respect when referring to or addressing her.)

I would also like to thank my wife, Elizabeth Zerweck-Tembo, and my children, Temwanani, Kamwendo, and Sekani, for their patience when I was away doing fieldwork and for their support when I was writing this book.

Lastly, I'd like to express my strongest heartfelt wish that Zambians and Africans of all persuasions document in the many media (audio, video, and print) available today our rich traditions, knowledge, and culture that are, as you read this, unfortunately rapidly going to waste in both urban and rural areas. The oral tradition is hardly a reliable medium for transmitting or storing traditional aspects of African culture, especially with the rapid onslaught of television and Westernization.

CONTENTS

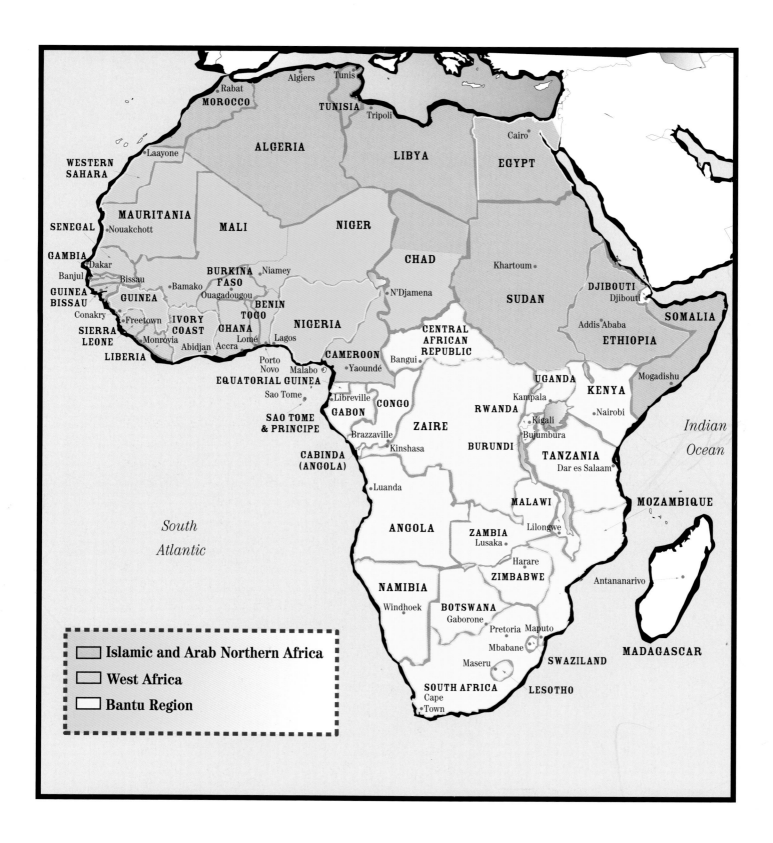

WESTERN
SAHARA

MOROCCO
Rabat

Algiers
TUNIS
Tunis

TUNISIA
Tripoli

ALGERIA

LIBYA

EGYPT
Cairo

Laayone

MAURITANIA

SENEGAL
Nouakchott

MALI

NIGER

CHAD

Khartoum

DJIBOUTI
Djibouti

GAMBIA
Dakar
Banjul
Bissau
GUINEA
BISSAU
Conakry

BURKINA
FASO
Niamey
Bamako
Ouagadougou

GUINEA
Freetown
IVORY
COAST
GHANA
Monrovia
Abidjan
Accra
Lomé
BENIN
TOGO

NIGERIA
Lagos

N'Djamena

SUDAN

Addis Ababa

SOMALIA

ETHIOPIA

SIERRA
LEONE

LIBERIA

Porto
Novo
Malabo
CAMEROON
Yaoundé

CENTRAL
AFRICAN
REPUBLIC
Bangui

Mogadishu

EQUATORIAL GUINEA
Sao Tome

Libreville
GABON
CONGO

UGANDA
Kampala
Kigali
RWANDA
Bujumbura
KENYA
Nairobi

SAO TOME
& PRINCIPE

Brazzaville
ZAIRE

Kinshasa

BURUNDI

TANZANIA
Dar es Salaam

CABINDA
(ANGOLA)

Luanda

MALAWI
Lilongwe

Indian
Ocean

MOZAMBIQUE

South

Atlantic

ANGOLA
ZAMBIA
Lusaka

Harare
ZIMBABWE
Antananarivo

NAMIBIA
Windhoek
BOTSWANA
Gaborone
Pretoria
Maputo
Mbabane
Maseru
SWAZILAND
MADAGASCAR

SOUTH AFRICA
Cape
Town
LESOTHO

Islamic and Arab Northern Africa

West Africa

Bantu Region

PREFACE

The expressions "African culture," "African attitudes," and "African mythology" are often used as inaccurate generalizations. This is because Africa is a huge continent, in fact more than three times the size of the United States. To give a more concrete idea, both China and India could fit into the African continent and there would be room left over. Africa has more than 680 million people living in diverse geographical, political, and social environments and speaking more than three thousand different indigenous languages. While a tiny minority of these people are still hunters and gatherers or nomads, the vast majority of Africans are subsistence farmers, pastoralists, urban dwellers, soldiers, educated elites, bureaucrats, or Westernized technocrats and even jet-setters.

For the purposes of contextualizing the mythology and folktales in this book, Africa can be divided into three regions: the predominantly Islamic and Arab Northern Africa; West Africa; and the Bantu region of Northeast, Central, and Southern Africa.

Despite the fact that Africa is a continent of great geographical and cultural diversity, myths from the different regions of the continent have a number of features and themes in common. These themes can be divided into several categories: some explain the creation of the earth, others examine the changing relationship between God and the world or deal with the origin of humanity, and others deal with birth and death. Legends and folktales tend to be extensions of these myths.

Although all African myths and folktales share similar characteristics, those in each region of Africa may have more distinctive patterns. For example, the most famous and revered character in West African mythology is Anansi the Spider. Among the Bantu of Central and Southern Africa, the Hare is famous for being conniving and for manipulating fellow animals as well as humans. Especially among African people in the Eastern Province of Zambia, Malawi, and parts of Mozambique, he is known as Kalulu.

INTRODUCTION TO AFRICAN MYTHS, FOLKTALES, AND LEGENDS

Many of the myths, folktales, and legends in this book played very important roles and achieved very distinct purposes in the lives of the African people. One of the most obvious purposes is that they often provided an explanation of the origins of a particular group or tribe. Different tribes answered the question "Where did we come from?" in different ways. Some believed that humans stemmed from their natural surroundings, while other tribes have more elaborate stories to explain their existence. These

Such structures as walls and window and door frames provide opportunities for artistic expression among many peoples of Africa. This is a Yoruba wooden door carved by Olowe of Ise in Nigeria.

11

Elders of the tribe always provided strong guidance to the young through customs, use of symbols, practicing of rituals, and traditional body adornment and dressing. Pictured here are young Masai girls with elders in traditional dress in Kenya.

creation myths are reflected in the peoples' beliefs and everyday mode of living.

As well as providing answers to fundamental questions of life and death, myths, folktales, and legends also served to instill moral values in the young people of the tribe or community. At the same time, the process of hearing or telling these tales reinforced and reiterated these values in the adults. These stories often taught the young that it was wrong to steal, murder, lie, or be self-centered or egotistical; they encouraged kindness and generosity to others, especially to orphaned children, the poor, and the disabled. The tales encouraged children to obey, help, and respect their parents and other elders, to be careful in choosing one's marriage partner, and to understand that bearing and raising children were two of the most important aspects of marriage.

Mythology, legends, and folktales in a traditional African cultural environment also teach children to be articulate—in any one of the possible thousands of African languages—when participating in the oral tradition of storytelling. This point may seem insignificant unless one realizes that children raised today have limited opportunities to achieve the level of oral articulation that existed when people relied on their oral tradition as a means of entertainment.

In a traditional agricultural African environment, tales are told at the end of the day. After a whole day's work in the fields, stories are told following supper. Confining the narration of folktales to evenings used to be a very strict custom. In fact, among the Tumbuka people of Eastern Zambia, children were warned that if they told folktales during the day, their mothers would turn into anthills.

The *Funk and Wagnalls Standard Dictionary of Folklore, Mythology, and Legend* confirms this: "It is widely felt that folktales are the special domain of the spirits of the dead, and that story-telling during the day will be punished." However, this taboo is no longer prevalent.

When adults and children sit around the fire, it is often a grandparent or an older member of the tribe who narrates the stories. Still, there are also many opportunities during the evenings for children to sit by themselves in the bright moonlight and take turns narrating folktales. Many of the folktales that appear in this book were collected by listening to children tell them to one another.

Many folktales have characters that sing during the narration; the audience is required to respond and participate in the singing of the songs. In a song, the main character is represented by the narrator, who leads the tale

Sculptors and carvers occupy very important positions in traditional Africa as they use their skill to represent many tribal symbols on wood and metal. Fonshu, a Nigerian sculptor, finishes an intricate-looking story piece.

The practice of body adornment as a symbol of femininity or masculinity starts at a very early age. Here, a Masai child is shown in her beautiful body adornments.

and instigates the audience to respond. As is characteristic of oral traditions, the details of most of the stories tend to differ depending on who tells them. A detail of the story "The Boy and His Dogs" may be offensive to adults but quite funny and silly to children. For example, in one variation of the story the protagonist farts as a means of defending himself against the boy's dogs. In the adult versions of the story the evil father may spit at the charging dogs or use a sharp piercing whistle instead.

To modern Western public sensibilities, which often demand political correctness, sensitivity, and cleanliness, some African folktales might appear crude, cruel, vulgar, and shocking. But life in much of traditional rural African culture was often unforgiving and still is somewhat even to this day. Vicious wars and ethnic strife continue to affect millions of Africans. For example, there are ongoing wars in southern Sudan between the Christian South and Muslim North, and in South Africa there are still racial and ethnic political conflicts. Disease, sudden and early childhood death, poverty, tribal wars, village and family conflicts and feuds, and danger from animals

and the oppressive elements of nature are all still part of life in Africa today. However, these same hostile environments also provide some of the most culturally satisfying, significant, vibrant, beautiful, enduring, and happy physical and social environments for the majority of African men, women, and children. A traditional African environment is still one of the most enduring sources of inspiration, community, cultural renewal, and continuity for most Africans, including myself. Many of the following myths, legends, and folktales reflect the multifaceted nature of this traditional African society.

One serious problem with African mythology is that it has been preserved only through the oral tradition, whereas stories from other parts of the world like Europe, India, China, and Japan have all been preserved in writing. Ali Mazrui, the world-renowned African scholar and presenter of the highly acclaimed Public Broadcasting Service series *The Africans*, said in his book *The Africans: A Triple Heritage* that most of black Africa had what he terms a weak or, in many cases, a lack of "archival tradition." As a result, "the scientific tradition became weak, sometimes our languages atrophied and so did philosophical tradition—with ghastly consequences for our people across the centuries." However, Geoffrey Parrinder, author of *African Mythology*, says, "Educated Africans also have now started to record the myths of their own people, before it is too late and they disappear or change."

In the few instances where African mythology has been written down, the stories were transcribed by European missionaries, who were very discriminating in their selections. The missionaries tended to record only stories that met their individual European expectations of what a folktale should be. They also recorded the stories using contemporary European standards of moral decency.

DEFINING
MYTHS,
LEGENDS, AND
FOLKTALES

Myths describe how things came to be and simultaneously explain how things have changed. They generally address spiritual issues and explain such mysteries as: How did the world come into being? How did men and women come to be? How did good and evil, animals, life and death, farmers, hunters and gatherers, pastoralists or herders, and fishermen all come about? Myths are usually considered sacred in every society and are regarded with awe, respect, and reverence by its members.

Legends are tales whose main characters are humans. In general, legends relate events that are more recent than those of myths. The audience and the narrator always regard legends as being true. While myths are regarded as being sacred, legends are regarded as profane, secular, or belonging to the ordinary world. Legends include narratives of wars, victories, significant or memorable deeds of leaders, ghosts, or saints; tales of buried treasure; and tragedies.

Folklore includes all the human knowledge, customs, and beliefs that have been passed down through the oral tradition. Folktales are fictional narratives that often relate the adventures of animals and humans involved in some dilemma.

Although myths are supposed to be products of human imagination, many scholars argue that their significance is not in whether they are false or true, but rather the major functions they play among human beings.

African mythology does provide the peoples of Africa with a very coherent way of explaining the origins of man and woman, family, birth, death, gender and sexuality, and their means of subsistence. Mythology also explains the nature of art, God, religion, and the supernatural, and how all these are related to man's fortunes and misfortunes. One can ar-

Masks, in their many varieties, depict and represent rituals and different life forces and forms. Masks may symbolize ancestral or evil spirits, femininity or masculinity, or power, and are used to conceal the dancer's identity in ritualistic and celebratory dances. This is a mask from the West African coastal region.

RIGHT: Paramount chiefs and wealthy heads of families have worn very expensive cloth, both locally woven and imported. The motifs embroidered on these cloths may represent significant aspects of a particular African people. Akan paramount chiefs of Ghana and other wealthy people wore this mill-woven embroidery-thread cloth known as *akunitam* ("cloth of the great"). Each symbol represents an important aspect of life or characters from folktales. For example, Anansi, the Spider, is in the upper left corner of this cloth.

BELOW: Drums are one of the most important artifacts of the African peoples. Drums' principal uses have been for dance and communication. This is a Yoruba drum from the Ife Ijebu area of Nigeria.

gue, then, that African mythology, although mostly still unwritten, is as effective as any set of beliefs insomuch as it creates a comprehensible worldview for its peoples.

If we define mythology as including myths, legends, and folktales, it not only explains human relationships to their natural surroundings, but also—and more importantly—provides models and patterns of human behavior and conduct. In his essay "Africa: Magic and Symbolism" in the book *Larousse World Mythology*, R. Bastide says, "Mythology provides man with models or patterns on which he must base his conduct, from the gesture of sowing seeds to the act of love, from house-building to the touch of fingers on the musical skin of the drum."

African myths, legends, and folktales are interrelated. Myths explain how things came to be, while legends and folktales tend to expand and reinforce in very direct ways some of the dominant myths of a particular African people. For example, if an African people has myths that pertain to the growing and cultivating of a staple crop, the folktales will not only incorporate the significance of the staple crop, but may also spell out the fortunes and

customs of the people related to it. For example, among the Buganda of Uganda, the myth of death involves a messenger bringing green bananas; bananas are an abundant food source in Uganda.

The myths, folktales, and legends that follow constitute a specific attempt at reinforcing and illustrating these links. These stories have very distinctive African characteristics, including the presence of tricksters, individ-

ual variation in the specific details of the tales, oral richness in the telling of the folktales (which can never really be appreciated when read), the significance of songs and singing in the folktales, and finally the explanatory elements of the folktales and legends.

Tricksters occur in tales from the West, East, Central, and Southern African peoples. The Hare is the most prominent trickster among peoples of East, Central, and Southern Africa. He is also important among the Jukun and Angass of Nigeria. The tortoise is a trickster among the Yoruba, Edo, and Ibo of Nigeria. Spider, known by his Twi name, Anansi, is the trickster in Liberia, Sierra Leone, and the Gold Coast. Often the trickster uses his mental powers rather than his physical ones to overcome an obstacle.

However, not all African folktales contain a trickster. Many others reinforce the moral

As a form of entertainment, village children dance, sing, and narrate folktales. These children are singing in the Okavango Delta in Botswana.

values of the people. For example, Africans still practice polygamy or more specifically polygyny. (Polygamy is a general term for the custom of one person having multiple marital partners, while polygyny is a more specific term used by anthropologists for the custom of men marrying more than one wife at the same time.) In their book *The Sociology of the African Family*, Diane Kayongo-Male and Philista Onyango suggest that the practice of polygyny is on the decline in Africa with the spreading of Westernization. They estimate that "the number of polygynists per 100 married men ranges from 20.4 to 36.4 in Benin, Chad, Congo, Gabon, Ghana, Kenya, Mali, Niger, Senegal, Tanzania, Togo, and Zaire.... Polygyny has been widely practiced in Africa, and it has important functions." Generally, in traditional communal village life, co-wives

live peacefully, and there are some folktales that discourage squabbling, envy, and jealousy. For example, a tale from the Hausa people of Nigeria tells of a woman who is jealous of her co-wife. The co-wife's child dies but is resurrected. The jealous woman kills her ugly child with the expectation that the child will be beautiful when resurrected. However, the child never comes back to life.

A characteristic that may be distinctive of a culture that has depended primarily on the oral tradition is that a folktale is never retold in exactly the same way. This may seem obvious, but European and other scholars may often search for an "accurate" story, one that is told exactly the same way by every member of the tribe or in every region of Africa. What the scholars may not realize is that verbal creativity is always present. No one story is going to be retold in exactly the same way; many of its features may be creatively modified by the narrator depending on the audience and the entire cultural environment. *Funk and Wagnalls* confirms this: "Variation is disconcerting only if one assumes that the only well-told tale is one memorized and recited word for word."

I noticed this creativity while conducting fieldwork among the Tumbuka tribe of Eastern Zambia. A man started telling the story "The Mysterious Bird" in a flat monotone. A woman took over the story halfway, adding enthusiasm, suspense, and such incredible humor that from time to time the audience was laughing itself silly with sheer joy. When the same woman led in the song, the melody was so soulful that it was clearly half the enjoyment in the telling of and listening to the folktale.

Songs and singing are an integral part of African folktales precisely because a song provides additional opportunities for the audience and the narrator to interact creatively and enjoy storytelling. This is one factor that makes reading African folktales such an inadequate experience. In a live experience, the narrator can improvise, use certain intonations for emphasis, be humorous, and use many other techniques to make the experience more rich. For example, repetition in African folktales denotes intensity. In the folktales in this book, expressions like "a long, long time ago," "he walked and walked," and "the bird flew, flew, flew" all denote intensity and duration of the activity. Reading folktales is like reading a play instead of watching it: the rich experience is missing.

Songs in African folktales are sometimes even more important than the tale being told. Among the Yoruba, if a narrator tries to cut short a favorite song, the audience might protest. Songs are in virtually all the folktales that follow, and many original recordings contained even more repetitions of the singing of the songs than are set down here. Repetition in African folktales, which may seem monotonous to Europeans or North Americans, can not only be explained in terms of emphasis, but also shows the high value placed on the actual song rather than the story itself. Good storytellers, therefore, may create additional occasions for singing well-liked songs, or they may be able to lengthen the story or shorten it depending on the mood of the audience. This is one of the reasons why a story heard within the context of an actual live African audience may be remarkably different from a story edited for publication. This is also why stories that are heard in an actual social setting may be different from those collected by an individual researcher.

Small figurines carved out of wood have many functions. They are sometimes used as fetishes and fertility symbols. These are twin male figures from the Yoruba people of Nigeria and an Akuaba figure from the Ashanti people of Ghana.

TRADITIONAL MYTHS

The Zulu of South Africa believe that the first man and woman came out of a reed. The Herero of Namibia believe that their ancestors were born out of a tree that still exists on their land, the veld. The Dinka of Sudan say that the first man and woman were molded out of clay and were at first very small. They were inserted into a pot, and when the pot was opened, they had grown larger. The Ashanti of Ghana, on the other hand, believe that the first humans came up from holes in the ground.

This mask from the coastal region of West Africa is used by men in traditional dances and rituals.

African creation mythology always involves a supreme being. In his book *African Mythology*, Geoffrey Parrinder comments that names for the supreme being vary according to specific languages in Africa, but that some names are common over larger areas. For example, Mulungu is used in East Africa and parts of Central Africa, specifically among the Chewa people of Zambia, Malawi, and parts of Mozambique, and has been adopted in about thirty different translations of the Bible into African languages. The Bemba of Northern Zambia and many tribes in Central Africa use Lesa. Nyambe is used in Botswana and the Congo region. In West Africa there are many names that are used, including Ngewo, Mawu, Amma, Olorum, and Chukwu.

The creation story of the Yoruba people of Nigeria tells that at the beginning of the world, the earth was a marshy swamp. Ol-rum, the supreme being, lived in and was the owner of the sky. There were no human beings yet. Then one day, Ol-rum summoned a junior god or deity, Orisha Nla, and told him that he wanted to create firm ground. Orisha Nla gave Ol-rum a snail shell in which there was some loose earth, a pigeon, and a hen with five toes. The supreme being threw the

Here are twin male figurines carved out of wood from the Yoruba people of Nigeria. Twins play a very significant role in the creation myths of many African peoples.

earth from the shell onto one small spot. Then he put the pigeon and the hen there. The hen and the pigeon scattered the earth, gradually spreading it to cover a wider and wider area and making the earth firm. Ol-rum sent the Chameleon to inspect the earth. The Chameleon returned and reported that the earth was now wide and dry. The place where creation started was called *Ife*, which means "wide." The word *Ile*, meaning "house," was later added. Ile-Ife has since been the most sacred city of the Yoruba people.

Among the Fon of Dahomey in West Africa, the supreme being is called Mawu. Mawu had a male twin named Lisa. The myth says that both twins were born from a more significant mother, Nana Buluku, who created the world and then retired.

Like myths around the world, African myths often serve both to explain and to justify the existence of certain traditional customs and rituals.

Myths about the origins of various means of subsistence and lifestyles are perhaps best represented by a Malagasy myth from what is today Madagascar. There were four men on earth who had separate means of subsistence but could not agree on anything. The first man was a hunter with a spear, the second was a trapper, the third was a fruit gatherer, and the fourth man worked in the soil. The four men decided to go to God to see if he could help them agree. When these men arrived, God was too busy pounding rice to talk to them. But he gave them each a handful of rice with instructions to sow it in three days.

The vast majority of Africans living in rural areas are subsistence agriculturists who use hoes to cultivate the land. It is estimated that women in traditional Africa contribute up to 80 percent of the total household labor involved in significant aspects of food production, preservation, processing, and storage. Here, a woman is tilling the land.

Hunting and gathering are the earliest documented means of subsistence among Africans. As modernization penetrates even the most remote parts of Africa, hunting as a sole means of life is disappearing. Here, two San (Bushmen) of the Kalahari Desert in Southern Africa are stalking game.

As they returned to their separate places, the first man saw some game. He dropped the rice and went hunting. The second heard a bird, put his rice down, and went to see the bird. When he came back the rice was gone. The third man, wanting to pick some fruit from a tree, accidentally dropped the rice in the river. The fourth put down the rice to dig the ground. The rice was blown and spread and grew all over. God concluded that the fates of the four men could not be changed. Each man from then on stuck to his fate: hunter, trapper, fruit gatherer, and farmer.

The creation myth among the Boshongo of Zaire, a Bantu tribe, is known as Bumba's Creation. At the beginning there was nothing but darkness and water. Bumba, the original man, was alone. Bumba vomited the sun,

then the leopard Koy Bumba, the crocodile Gunda Bumba, and several other creatures. Last to be vomited were other men. David Leeming, a scholar of world mythology, says in his book *The World of Myth*, "There were many men, but only one was white like Bumba. His name was Loko Yima." Leeming further says, "The absence of the female principle here suggests a patrilineal culture. The fact that Bumba is white suggests that this is a late myth, affected, like so much African mythology, by the presence of the white race in colonial Africa."

A common notion in African creation myths is that in the beginning, God, the sky, and the earth were very close together. During this period humans had a blissful, easy life. Some tribes say that when people were hun-

African women spend most of the day processing and cooking food for their families. Women spend many hours pounding grains (millet and maize) using a pestle and mortar to make flour or mealie-meal for their family's food.

gry, they just reached up to the sky and ate a piece. Parrinder says that "the sky was low and hung just above men's heads. This led to undue familiarity; children wiped greasy hands on the sky after meals, and women tore bits off the sky for cooking." Angered by human negligence, selfishness, and greed, God moved away from humans. Among the Dinka people of the Sudan, for example, the myth says that when a greedy woman who wanted to make more food than she needed hit the sky with her pestle, God became very angry. From that day, humans have had to work hard for their food, are often hungry, cannot reach God easily, and have been victims of illness and death. In the majority of the incidents leading to God's ire, a woman was the offending party. The fact that women are consistently identified as the ones that offended God reflects the possibility that men often told the myths.

The Fon people of Dahomey believe that God once lived very close to the earth and that the trickster Legba had a very close relationship with him. Whenever God did something that was harmful to man, God always blamed it on Legba. God could do this since Legba had a reputation with man for getting into mischief. However, Legba got tired and resented the situation. He convinced an old woman to always throw her dirty water into the sky after she washed. God was annoyed at the water being constantly thrown into his face and he gradually moved away to his present distance. But Legba was left behind and that is why he has a shrine in every house and village, to report on human doings to God. This theme of humans living blissfully until

they angered God is common in the creation myths of the Ivory Coast, Ghana, Togo in West Africa, Nuba in the Sudan, and the Lozi of Zambia, and among the Pygmies of the Congo rain forest.

In African mythology, there are many accounts of struggles between death and the first men. There are often deceptions, delays, tardiness, conceit, and anger between the supreme being and man that result in the beginning of death. The Kono people of Sierra Leone say that there was once a first man and woman and their baby. The supreme being told them that they would never die. Instead, when they grew old, they would be given new skin. The supreme being gave the new skins in a bundle to the Dog and sent it to give it to the man. On the way, the Dog met other animals that were feasting on rice and pumpkins. He put the bundle down and joined in the

Daily chores for rural women and girls include drawing water for bathing, drinking, and cooking.

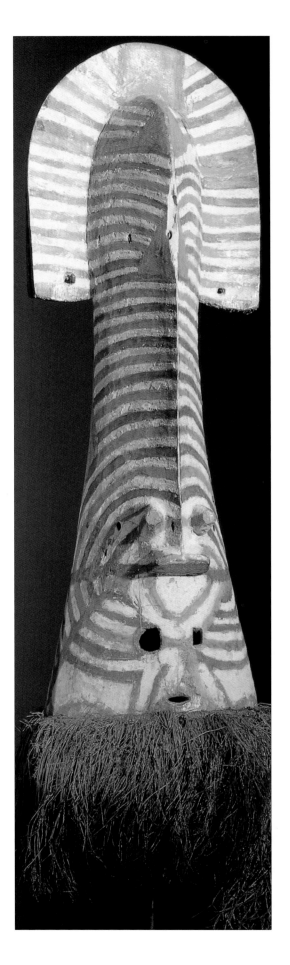

Masks are used in many ceremonies and celebrations. This is the *Mwadi* helmet mask used in "dance of the new moon" at funeral and marriage celebrations along the Lomani River in Zaire.

feast. The animals asked what was in the bag. The Dog explained that the bundle contained new skins. The animals did not pay much attention to this information, but the Snake overheard the conversation. He sneaked up, stole the bundle of new skins, and gave them to his friends. The Dog went to report about the stolen new skins to the supreme being, but it was too late. The Snake kept the skins and people have died since then.

Among the Zulu and Xhosa Bantu tribes of South Africa, the dominant figure in creation mythology is Unkulunkulu, "the Very Old." This is the first man, or ancestor of the human race. He is also responsible for death. He sent the slow Chameleon with the message to humans that they would not die. However, the Chameleon took too long delivering it and Unkulunkulu became angry and impatient. He sent the fast Lizard with the message for the Chameleon to tell men that death would come. The role of the slow Chameleon is a common theme in African creation mythology, particularly among the Bantu tribes.

Among the Buganda, the first man, Kintu, and his wife, Nambi, lived happily in the sky. Then the supreme being sent them to live on earth. As they were leaving the sky, Kintu and Nambi were told by the supreme being, Gulu, not to return for any reason, because then Death would want to come with them. However, Nambi returned to get some grain that they had forgotten to bring for the goats and fowls they had taken with them. Death then followed them to earth. Man tried to elude and fight Death but to no avail. Since that time men have died.

The Chewa people of Eastern Zambia have a myth about the origin of death involving the famous trickster Kalulu, the Hare, and the slow Chameleon. This myth is retold in a short book of folktales collected by J. Brewer, a Dutch missionary, in 1947, in the Fort James district, which is now called Chipata, in Eastern Zambia. Entitled *Kalulu ndi Nyama Zinzace* (*Hare and His Brother Animals*), the book was originally published in the ChiNyanja or, as it is also called, ChiChewa indigenous African language. The myth is a variation of a similar one from the Xhosa and Zulu people of South Africa. God called the Chameleon to the sky and sent him to tell human beings that although people were suffering death, they would come back from the dead and be alive again. The Chameleon learned the message by heart and began his journey to earth. On his way he met Kalulu, who asked him when he would reach his home as he was walking so slowly. Chameleon said he was taking a message from God to the people on earth.

Kalulu asked what the message was. When Chameleon told it to the Hare, Kalulu begged and insisted that he be allowed to rush ahead with the message. He said he had heard people mourning only the previous day because someone had died. The people would be very happy to hear the good message from God. Chameleon reluctantly agreed but cautioned Kalulu not to forget the message. Kalulu ran really fast with God's message. But in his haste, Kalulu forgot the actual message and instead said, "God says to you people 'Although you are suffering with life, you will also have death.'" By the time the slow Chameleon had arrived, Kalulu's wrong message had already cast the misfortune of death on the whole earth.

In addition to dealing with the origins of life and the reality of death, myths explain many of the features of the environment. There are myths from the Ila people of Zambia, for example, that explain shortages of food and how humans came to be fated to a life of suffering and of struggle for existence. A myth from Malagasy explains the origin of rice. There are also myths that explain the origin of fire among the Pygmies of the Congo rain forests and the Dogon of Mali.

The chameleon is well known for its ability to change colors and particularly for its slow speed. It is incorporated into many African myths, especially those concerned with the origin of death.

CHAPTER

II

FOLKTALES

The folktales that follow have songs in them. The songs are written in the
original Tumbuka language, with the translated or partially translated version of the same stanza in parentheses. Some of the Tumbuka words in the
lyrics of the songs have not been translated into English as the equivalent
is not known or does not exist. The songs, as mentioned previously, are enacted
in a call-and-response format with the narrator representing the main character
in the story.

The Marca (or Marka) are a fishing people in
the San district of Mali. This is a Marca tribal
mask made of metal from Mali in West Africa.

31

THE BOY
AND HIS DOGS

Once upon a time, there was a man who married a very beautiful woman. The woman bore him several healthy babies. But each time one was born, the husband, who was an extremely evil man, would roast and eat the baby while his wife was away drawing water from the river. The woman was always angry and disappointed, for she had no children.

But one day she gave birth to a baby boy and had an idea. She decided to hide the baby away so that her husband could not see him. So the woman hid the baby away in the bush in the hollow trunk of a large baobab tree. Every day she stole away secretly to feed the baby. When her husband angrily asked her where she went and what she was doing in the bush every day, she would lie and tell him

that she had been to the river to fetch water, mushrooms, or firewood. She did this until the baby grew into a big boy.

Since the child was now big, she decided to bring him home, as her husband would not be able to eat him. She told her husband that the boy was their child and that she had hidden him from the time he was born. The husband still wanted to eat the boy, but he did not show it. Instead he patted the boy on the head and told him he was a big strong boy.

The young boy had four lovely trusted dogs with which he used to go hunting in the bush. The boy named his four dogs *Cimthiko* (cooking stick), *Kanyalubwe* (leopard), *Chinkhali* (large cooking pot), and *Cimbelu* (bell). He took the dogs with him wherever he went. At night the dogs slept at the boy's four sides: one near his head, one at his feet, one at his left side, and one at his right side. During several nights, as the boy lay sound asleep, the

Drought-resistant baobab trees are very common in regions of Africa with a savannah grassland climate and vegetation. Baobab trees often have big hollows, like these in Hwange in Zimbabwe.

wicked father put a big axe into the hot embers of the fire until it grew red-hot and glowed in the dark. He raised it over the boy's neck to strike him. But the dogs angrily growled and barked at him, at which point the boy woke up, rubbing his eyes. The father quickly hid the axe and slid under his covers, pretending to be asleep. So although the father wanted to eat the boy, he could not find a good opportunity to do so.

One day the father managed to persuade the boy to go with him to the forest to fetch some honey. The boy whistled for his four dogs to come along, but the father convinced him that they would not need them. So they set off for the bush carrying only an axe. As honeybees often make their hives up in the hollows of tall trees, they would use the axe for chopping down the tree.

They searched and searched for a long time until they found that some bees had nested at the tip of a very tall and big tree. The father immediately told his son to climb the tree. When the boy was halfway up the tree, the man shouted in a deep, evil voice:

"This is the end of you!! I am going to kill and eat you today!!!"

The boy was afraid and cried as the man began to chop down the big tree with his axe. After a while, the boy began to sing a song:

NARRATOR: *Chinkhali nyalilo*

AUDIENCE: *A e e e e nyalilo*

NARRATOR: *Nchebe yane nyalilo*
(My dog)

AUDIENCE: *A e e e e nyalilo*

NARRATOR: *Zanga kuno nyalilo*
(Come here)

AUDIENCE: *A e e e e nyalilo*

NARRATOR: *Bakomane nyalilo* (He is
going to kill me)

AUDIENCE: *A e e e e nyalilo*

As the man chopped the tree, he replied to the boy's song:

THE MAN: *Waliwa lelo waliwa* (You
will be killed today, you will be
killed)

AUDIENCE: *Waliwa lelo waliwa*
(You will be killed today,
you will be killed)

When the boy's dog Chinkhali heard the song, he knew his master was in danger in the forest. He whined, perked up his ears, and dashed through the forest to where the song was coming from. As the trunk of the tree was very large, the man had only chopped away a small portion of it. When the angry dog approached him, the man farted loudly and the dog died instantly. The boy in the tree was disappointed and afraid. Then he sang the same song again and again, calling for his dogs Cimthiko and Cimbelu. But both these dogs also died when the man farted.

By now the boy was really desperate. His hopes of rescue lay in his last dog, Kanyalubwe. By this time the man had chopped most of the big tree trunk and soon it was going to fall over. The boy sang his song:

NARRATOR: *Kanyalubwe nyalilo*

AUDIENCE: *A e e e e nyalilo*

NARRATOR: *Nchebe yane nyalilo*
(My dog)

AUDIENCE: *A e e e e nyalilo*

Fathers and sons have close relationships and often perform men's jobs, like hunting, together in traditional society. Here a San (Bushman) in Namibia is teaching his young son how to make fire.

While the men and boys of the Masai tribe in Kenya go far afield to graze domestic animals like goats and cattle, the women stay home in the village to cook and to look after and nurture children, the sick, and the elderly.

NARRATOR: *Zanga kuno nyalilo*
(Come here)

AUDIENCE: *A e e e e nyalilo*

NARRATOR: *Bakomane nyalilo*
(He is going to kill me)

AUDIENCE: *A e e e e nyalilo*

As the man chopped the tree, he replied to the boy's song:

THE MAN: *Waliwa lelo waliwa* (You will be killed today, you will be killed)

AUDIENCE: *Waliwa lelo waliwa* (You will be killed today, you will be killed)

When the boy's dog Kanyalubwe heard the song, he knew his master was in danger in the forest. He dashed through the forest, through the underbrush, growling and barking. As the charging, angry dog approached the place, the man farted loudly again and again. But just as the leopard is angry and undeterred, the angry dog continued to charge with great force and speed. He attacked the man and tore him into pieces. The boy quickly climbed down to safety just as the tree was about to fall over.

The boy looked around the forest and collected some herbs from a special tree. He used the herbs to revive his three dead dogs. The boy then returned home to the village. The boy, his mother, and the four dogs lived happily ever after.

THE MYSTERIOUS BIRD

A long time ago, a man named Cavura set out on a journey from his village. He walked and traveled by bus for a long distance to many large cities in search of a job. After he found a job he worked for a long time and saved his money. He bought many wonderful gifts and presents, then decided to return home to his village. He walked and walked on a path for a long time, passing many villages where people admired his many beautiful gifts.

As he continued on his journey, two men spotted the traveler and admired his nice belongings. They murdered the poor man, stole his gifts and presents, and hid his body in the cikuyu tree, which had very thick leaves. What the men did not know was that a little bird had seen them. The two men carried the goods as their own. When they arrived at one village, the people wondered and asked, "Where did you get all these nice things from? Eh! eh! Look at all these shirts and blankets, and the suitcase and the radio!"

"Well," the men hesitated, "we were kind of walking along hunting and we found them abandoned in the bush."

Still puzzled, the village people welcomed the two men as their guests. As the men sat, the little bird began to sing in a tree nearby:

> NARRATOR: *Ati adada vura yakoma kanyangali* (Cavura is dead)
>
> AUDIENCE: *Kanyangali ya kanyangali*
>
> NARRATOR: *A Cavura bakoma kanyangali* (Cavura has been killed)
>
> AUDIENCE: *Kanyangali ya kanyangali*
>
> NARRATOR: *Awe yakoma yakoma kanyangali* (Oh, poor soul, he was killed)
>
> AUDIENCE: *Kanyangali ya kanyangali*
>
> NARRATOR: *Awe yakoma yakoma kanyangali* (Oh, poor soul, he was killed)
>
> AUDIENCE: *Kanyangali ya kanyangali*
>
> NARRATOR: *Ati adada vura yakoma kanyangali* (Cavura was killed)
>
> AUDIENCE: *Kanyangali ya kanyangali*

> NARRATOR: *Adada vura yakoma kanyangali* (Cavura was killed)
>
> AUDIENCE: *Kanyangali ya kanyangali*
>
> NARRATOR: *Bakomera mucikuyu kanyangali* (They killed him under a cikuyu tree)
>
> AUDIENCE: *Kanyangali ya kanyangali*
>
> NARRATOR: *Cikuyu cobendama kanyangali* (A cikuyu tree that is bent)
>
> AUDIENCE: *Kanyangali ya kanyangali*
>
> NARRATOR: *Awe bakoma bakoma kanyangali* (Oh, poor soul, they have killed him)
>
> AUDIENCE: *Kanyangali ya kanyangali*
>
> NARRATOR: *Awe bakoma bakoma kanyangali* (Oh, poor soul, they have killed him)
>
> AUDIENCE: *Kanyangali ya kanyangali*
>
> (Repeat two times)

This Yoruba wooden carving of a male figure dressed in intricately embroidered dress is an example of the artistic skill of the Yoruba people.

The people in the village were amazed. "Listen to what the little bird is singing," they said. "Listen very carefully." The people were quiet and the little bird began to sing again:

NARRATOR: *Ati adada vura yakoma kanyangali* (Cavura was killed)

AUDIENCE: *Kanyangali ya kanyangali*

NARRATOR: *Adada vura yakoma kanyangali* (Cavura was killed)

AUDIENCE: *Kanyangali ya kanyangali*

NARRATOR: *Bakomera mucikuyu kanyangali* (They killed him under a cikuyu tree)

AUDIENCE: *Kanyangali ya kanyangali*

NARRATOR: *Cikuyu cobendama kanyangali* (A cikuyu tree that is bent)

AUDIENCE: *Kanyangali ya kanyangali*

NARRATOR: *Awe bakoma bakoma kanyangali* (Oh, poor soul, they have killed him)

AUDIENCE: *Kanyangali ya kanyangali*

NARRATOR: *Awe bakoma bakoma kanyangali* (Oh, poor soul, they have killed him)

Transportation is always a problem in rural Africa. Here, two men on bicycles carry valuable merchandise between villages near Mansa district in the Luapula Province of rural Zambia.

AUDIENCE: *Kanyangali ya*
kanyangali

(Repeat)

After it had finished the song, the little bird flew and flapped its wings and very deliberately landed next to the guests. The two men panicked and knew they were in trouble if they did not do something. One of the men grabbed the little bird and shoved it in his pocket. Excusing himself as if he was going to urinate, the man went to the bush. He killed the little bird and ground it into the dirt. He picked up the dirt and threw it into a deep hole and buried it.

The man returned from the bush with obvious relief and sat down. The two killers were anticipating a delicious meal of chicken and other assorted foods as guests of the village. Shortly afterward, however, the little bird came back from the dead and landed on the rooftop of one of the houses. The bird began to sing again:

NARRATOR: *Ati adada vura yakoma*
kanyangali (Cavura was killed)

AUDIENCE: *Kanyangali ya*
kanyangali

NARRATOR: *Adada vura yakoma*
kanyangali (Cavura was killed)

AUDIENCE: *Kanyangali ya*
kanyangali

NARRATOR: *Bakomera mucikuyu*
kanyangali (They killed him
under a cikuyu tree)

AUDIENCE: *Kanyangali ya*
kanyangali

NARRATOR: *Cikuyu cobendama*
kanyangali (A cikuyu tree
that is bent)

AUDIENCE: *Kanyangali ya*
kanyangali

NARRATOR: *Awe bakoma bakoma*
kanyangali (Oh, poor soul,
they have killed him)

AUDIENCE: *Kanyangali ya*
kanyangali

NARRATOR: *Awe bakoma bakoma*
kanyangali (Oh, poor soul,
they have killed him)

AUDIENCE: *Kanyangali ya*
kanyangali

(Repeat)

There was consternation in the village. "This bird keeps singing that they killed a Mr. Cavura," the people said among themselves.

The people decided to confront the two men. "You killed this little bird and it came back from the dead persisting with the same

BELOW: Carving of an ancestor figure from Guinea Bissau in West Africa.

RIGHT: A bat-eared fox in the Ngorongoro Crater of Tanzania. Bat-eared foxes are mostly nocturnal and feed on insects, scorpions, and birds' eggs, but the folktales have the Fox eating cow peas.

song about having witnessed someone's being murdered. Did you murder anyone by the name of Cavura?" the people asked.

The two men finally confessed that they had murdered someone and stolen all his expensive belongings. The people followed the little bird, as it flew and sang, leading all the way to where the body was hidden. The body was found hidden in the thick cikuyu tree. That's the end.

KALULU
THE HARE
AND
THE FOX

A long, long time ago, Kalulu the Hare and the Fox were great friends. They ate, played, and did everything together. One day the two friends were very hungry and decided to go and steal some cow peas. In the middle of the night, they sneaked into a farmer's field and ate some of his delicious cow peas. When the farmer arrived in his field the following morning, he was angry to find that some of his cow peas had been eaten. The farmer did not know what to do. Kalulu and the Fox liked the cow peas so much that they went to the field every night to eat.

One day, the farmer decided to set some traps to catch the animals that were eating his cow pea crop. When Kalulu and the Fox sneaked into the farmer's field that night, they were both caught in a trap. They were afraid of what the farmer was going to do to them once they were found the next day. Then Kalulu had an idea.

"Fox," Kalulu said, "If we pretend to be dead by lying still, the farmer will untie us from the trap and then we can run away."

The Fox agreed, and the two practiced playing dead. Kalulu lay still, held his breath and pretended not to breathe, opened his eyes wide without blinking, and did not twitch. But when the Fox tried to play dead, he could not do it. The Fox could hold his breath for only a few seconds before he began hyperventilating, making small, jerky moaning sounds.

"I can't do it, Kalulu, I can't," complained the Fox.

"You'd better do it because the farmer will be here soon after sunrise," replied Kalulu.

The Fox tried several times, but failed. After sunrise, the farmer arrived to inspect his field. As the farmer walked toward them, Kalulu urged the Fox to play dead, as the farmer was going to be there any second now. Kalulu then turned limp and played dead. His breathing was not noticeable; his eyes were wide open and ants crawled into them, but he did not flinch. Meanwhile, his friend the Fox was still hyperventilating when he tried to stop breathing for only a few seconds. The Fox tried to open his eyes wide without blinking, but he could not stop blinking when ants crawled in his eyes nor keep from swatting at the flies as they bothered him.

The farmer was happy that the two had been caught in his trap. He took one look at Kalulu and said to himself, "This one is already dead. I do not have to do anything." When he looked at the Fox, he was not fooled. The farmer said to himself, pointing at the Fox, "He is not yet dead; I will finish him off." The farmer killed the Fox. He then untied both of them from the trap.

The farmer had a young son. "Son," the farmer said, "take these two animals to the village. Give them to your mother and tell her to cook them for dinner."

The boy walked toward the village, carrying the two animals. Halfway to the village, Kalulu suddenly woke up. The boy was very startled.

"Where are you taking us?" Kalulu asked.

"Well," the boy replied, "my father told me that I should take you to the village and give you to my mother who will cook you for our dinner."

"No, no, no," protested Kalulu. "You did not listen correctly. Your father said to tell your mother to cook the Fox but to prepare me a warm bath, and cook a delicious meal made from that big rooster for me."

When they arrived in the village, the boy did as Kalulu had asked and told his mother to cook the Fox for his father for dinner, but to prepare a warm bath and cook that big rooster for Kalulu to eat. The boy's mother followed the boy's instructions. Kalulu had a warm bath and was served a very big delicious meal, which he ate to his satisfaction. Afterward Kalulu asked if he could take a nap with the sleeping baby. He crawled under the covers with the baby, both of them covered from head to toe, and fell fast asleep.

When the farmer returned from the fields late in the afternoon, he was very tired and hungry and expected a delicious meal. He greeted his wife and asked whether the dinner of the two animals was ready.

"Two animals?" asked the wife. "Our son said to cook the Fox and provide a warm bath and cook a delicious meal with the big rooster for Kalulu!"

The farmer knew that they had been tricked and demanded to know where Kalulu was. She said that he was taking a nap with the baby. The farmer was angry and was now going to take care of Kalulu once and for all. He whispered to his wife to point out where Kalulu was sleeping under the covers. What they did not know was that Kalulu had overheard the whole conversation. So he had switched places with the baby. When the farmer struck, he hit his own baby. Kalulu bounded out of the covers and ran out of the house into the bush as fast as possible.

An Epa masquerade mask of the Yoruba people of Nigeria.

A woman tending to the brewing of a traditional non-alcoholic beverage in Ghana in West Africa.

KASIWA
AND NGOZA

A long, long time ago, a man and a woman were married. They had two children, both girls, whose names were Kasiwa and Ngoza. One day the father fell gravely ill and died. A few months later the mother also fell sick. On her deathbed, she said to her younger daughter, Kasiwa:

"Kasiwa my daughter, I am about to die. When I am dead, you go and live with your older sister, Ngoza. She will look after you."

Ngoza, the older sister, was married. After their mother died, Ngoza took her sister Kasiwa into her household. But Ngoza was very cruel. Whenever she cooked the *nshima* meal, she ate all the good nshima food. (*Nshima* is the traditional Zambian staple food which Zambians eat at least twice a day—at lunch and supper. It is made by cooking cornmeal in hot water and stirring the contents until they are thick. It is always served with a second dish, which might be beans, meat, or vegetables.) But for her sister, Kasiwa, she made bad nshima cooked out of coarse corn husks and served with maggots. Ngoza served the meal in an old, dirty, broken gourd and Kasiwa had to eat on her own, behind the *nkhokwe* near the bushes.

This went on for a long time. One day Kasiwa decided to go to her mother's grave. Once she was there, Kasiwa began to sing:

NARRATOR: *Akuti fya mbalame*
(Shoo, birds, go away)

AUDIENCE: *Kacenjerekete kacenjerekete ya*

NARRATOR: *Fya mbalame*
(Birds, go away)

AUDIENCE: *Kacenjerekete kacenjerekete ya*

NARRATOR: *Amana bakalaila we*
(Mother bid me farewell)

AUDIENCE: *Kacenjerekete kacenjerekete ya*

NARRATOR: *Para namkufwa ine*
(When I die)

AUDIENCE: *Kacenjerekete kacenjerekete ya*

NARRATOR: *Uye kumkulu wako* (Go and live with your older sister)

AUDIENCE: *Kacenjerekete kacenjerekete ya*

NARRATOR: *Mukulu wako ni Ngoza*
(Your older sister, Ngoza)

AUDIENCE: *Kacenjerekete kacenjerekete ya*

NARRATOR: *Khukhu*

AUDIENCE: *Mwana wanga wasauka*
(My daughter is suffering)

NARRATOR: *Khukhu*

AUDIENCE: *Mwana wanga wasauka*
(My daughter is suffering)

Nothing happened and the graveyard was very quiet and eerie. Kasiwa sang the song again. After she finished singing the song, her mother's grave suddenly cracked open. Her mother came out of the grave. She took one look at her daughter and said, "Oh! Oh! My poor daughter. You are so very, very thin and haggard. Do you eat nshima?"

"No, mother," Kasiwa sobbed. "My sister Ngoza cooks me nshima from corn husks served with maggots in an old, dirty, broken gourd. She tells me to eat by myself near the bush behind the nkhokwe."

"I cannot believe this!" replied her mother. "Oh, poor thing! Come with me."

She took her daughter Kasiwa into the grave. Kasiwa was so happy to see her mother that she became really sassy. Kasiwa sang:

NARRATOR: *Akuti amama sima amama sima* (Mother nshima, mother nshima)

AUDIENCE: *Songa mbilibili*

NARRATOR: *Amama sima amama sima* (Mother nshima, mother nshima)

AUDIENCE: *Songa mbilibili*

NARRATOR: *Leka nkhuphikire mwana wane iwe* (Let me cook you the nshima, my daughter)

AUDIENCE: *Songa mbilibili*

NARRATOR: *Chizaso chinthu ici cakoma ine* (Come again, whatever killed me)

The majority of African people bury their dead in graves dug in the ground. The Dogon people of Mali, however, live in very rocky environments; since it is impossible to dig, the Dogon entomb their dead in holes in the cliffs.

Kasiwa's mother cooked a very delicious nshima. Then Kasiwa sang another song:

NARRATOR: *Akuti amama niliskeni amama niliskeni* (Mother, will you feed me, will you feed me)

AUDIENCE: *Songa mbilibili*

NARRATOR: *Amama niliskeni amama niliskeni* (Will you feed me, will you feed me)

AUDIENCE: *Songa mbilibili*

NARRATOR: *Leka nkhuliske mwana wane iwe* (Let me feed you, let me feed you, my daughter)

AUDIENCE: *Songa mbilibili*

NARRATOR: *Chizaso cinthu ici cankoma ine* (Come again, whatever killed me)

AUDIENCE: *Songa mbilibili*

Kasiwa's mother fed her, gave her a nice bath, and combed her hair. She gave Kasiwa everything she wanted, including a new dress. As it was getting dark, Kasiwa's mother said, "My daughter, it is getting dark. Let me escort you home."

"Yes, mother," answered Kasiwa.

The two walked along a path until they reached a tree. From there Kasiwa walked alone to the village as her mother watched her. Kasiwa arrived in the village as quietly as possible as dusk fell. But Ngoza saw her.

"Look at this little bad child that is always wandering around aimlessly," Ngoza said scornfully. "Where have we been, eh?"

Kasiwa sat quietly and did not say anything to her sister.

"Who bought you these new clothes?" another person asked. "No one in the village can afford any clothes, but where did you get new clothes since you are a helpless orphan?"

Ngoza demanded the new clothes and took them away. Kasiwa sat helplessly. She was given the bad nshima cooked out of corn husks and served with maggots, and was told to go eat near the bush. Kasiwa took the nshima and walked away, dumping the food when no one was looking. She came back with the empty, dirty, old, broken piece of gourd on which the food had been served and put it away.

The poor on the outskirts of the cities of Africa often manage to improve their conditions by building brick houses. These are an improvement over the traditional houses, which are built principally with poles made from trees, mud, and grass roofs.

"Did you really eat all that food so quickly?" Ngoza asked.

"Yes," lied Kasiwa. "I ate it all."

"You liar," Ngoza said. "You didn't even eat the food. You threw it away." Kasiwa sat quietly.

They went to bed. The following day, Kasiwa was told to work around the house all day. In the late afternoon she sneaked away to go and see her mother again at the grave.

There she sang the song:

NARRATOR: *Akuti fya mbalame*
(Shoo, birds, go away)

AUDIENCE: *Kacenjerekete kacenjerekete ya*

NARRATOR: *Fya mbalame*
(Birds, go away)

AUDIENCE: *Kacenjerekete kacenjerekete ya*

NARRATOR: *Amana bakalaila we*
(Mother bid me farewell)

AUDIENCE: *Kacenjerekete kacenjerekete ya*

NARRATOR: *Para namkufwa ine*
(When I die)

AUDIENCE: *Kacenjerekete kacenjerekete ya*

NARRATOR: *Uye kumkulu wako* (Go and live with your older sister)

AUDIENCE: *Kacenjerekete kacenjerekete ya*

NARRATOR: *Mukulu wako ni Ngoza*
(Your older sister, Ngoza)

AUDIENCE: *Kacenjerekete kacenjerekete ya*

NARRATOR: *Khukhu*

AUDIENCE: *Mwana wanga wasauka*
(My daughter is suffering)

NARRATOR: *Khukhu*

AUDIENCE: *Mwana wanga wasauka*
(My daughter is suffering)

Huge cracks appeared on the grave. Kasiwa's mother came out and took her daugh-

A woman of the Rendile tribe of the East African country of Kenya.

ter into the grave. She cooked delicious food for her daughter, gave her a bath, and gave her new clothes. As darkness fell, Kasiwa's mother escorted her to the tree again. Back in the village, Kasiwa was subjected to the same bad treatment again. The following day, she went again to the grave to see her mother and then returned to the same scornful treatment. This went on for several days.

One day, the people began to wonder where it was Kasiwa went to that she always came back looking so clean. And where did

A wooden carving
depicting an adult
and a child of the
Myombe peoples of
the Bakongo region.

she get all those new clothes? Who bought them for her? The villagers decided to follow her. They hid in the bushes until they saw her arrive at her mother's grave. Then, Kasiwa began to sing:

> NARRATOR: *Akuti fya mbalame*
> (Shoo, birds, go away)
>
> AUDIENCE: *Kacenjerekete kacenjerekete ya*
>
> NARRATOR: *Fya mbalame*
> (Birds, go away)
>
> AUDIENCE: *Kacenjerekete kacenjerekete ya*
>
> NARRATOR: *Amana bakalaila we*
> (Mother bid me farewell)
>
> AUDIENCE: *Kacenjerekete kacenjerekete ya*
>
> NARRATOR: *Para namkufwa ine*
> (When I die)
>
> AUDIENCE: *Kacenjerekete kacenjerekete ya*
>
> NARRATOR: *Uye kumkulu wako* (Go and live with your older sister)
>
> AUDIENCE: *Kacenjerekete kacenjerekete ya*
>
> NARRATOR: *Mukulu wako ni Ngoza*
> (Your older sister, Ngoza)
>
> AUDIENCE: *Kacenjerekete kacenjerekete ya*
>
> NARRATOR: *Khukhu*
>
> AUDIENCE: *Mwana wanga wasauka*
> (My daughter is suffering)
>
> NARRATOR: *Khukhu*
>
> AUDIENCE: *Mwana wanga wasauka*
> (My daughter is suffering)

The grave cracked open and Kasiwa's mother came out. She took Kasiwa into the grave, cooked her food, fed her, gave her a nice bath, combed her hair, and dressed her in new clothes. When the time came for Kasiwa to return to the village, the people hiding in the bushes, who had seen all of this, came out and caught the two.

The villagers confronted Kasiwa's mother. "So you died a long time ago but you are the one who has been caring for this girl! You should come back and live in the village."

"No," Kasiwa's mother refused. "I cannot come back to live in the village. I died many years ago. I live in the bush in the grave."

But the villagers persisted in urging her to come back to the village. At last Kasiwa's mother gave in.

"If you want me to come back and live in the village," she said, "give me six cows."

The villagers gave her six cows and Kasiwa's mother came back to the village and they lived happily ever after.

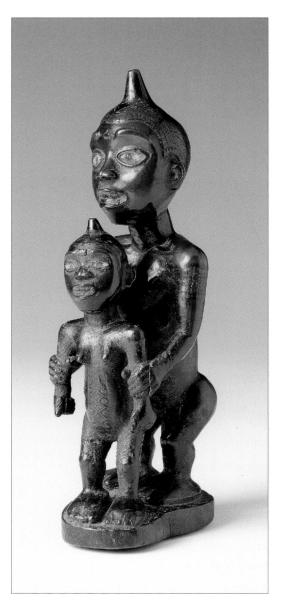

THE BIG BIRD AND HER CHILDREN

A long time ago there was a very big bird who was crippled and had only one leg, one wing, and one eye. The bird had five children. She loved and helped four of the five children, but the fifth child was very insolent. He was stubborn and belligerent, and did not show any respect to his mother at all. In fact, he would refuse to run errands and even denied that the bird was really his mother because she was crippled.

One day the bird told all her children that they were going to move and build a new nest far away. The new nest was going to be located beyond the big river. Although the bird was crippled and had only one leg, one wing, and one eye, she was going to carry all her children over the big river one at a time. So she began by carrying the first child. She instructed each child to sing a song as they were flying to the new nest. The child sang:

> NARRATOR: *Kanyangali nyangali nyangali* (Let me hold on to the feathers so I won't drown)
>
> AUDIENCE: *Kanyangali ya kanyangali*
>
> NARRATOR: *Kanyangali nyangali nyangali* (Let me hold on to the feathers so I won't drown)
>
> AUDIENCE: *Kanyangali ya kanyangali*

The big bird flapped its big wing—flap! flap! flap!—until it arrived at the very middle of the big river where it could not see either riverbank. The child sang:

> NARRATOR: *Kanyangali nyangali nyangali* (Let me hold on to the feathers so I won't drown)
>
> AUDIENCE: *Kanyangali ya kanyangali*

A mud painting done on a hand-woven cotton cloth in the Ivory Coast.

NARRATOR: *Kanyangali nyangali nyangali* (Let me hold on to the feathers so I won't drown)

AUDIENCE: *Kanyangali ya kanyangali*

The big bird flapped, flapped, and flapped until it landed and put down the first child. The bird returned and picked up the second child. As it began crossing the big river again, the child sang:

NARRATOR: *Kanyangali nyangali nyangali* (Let me hold on to the feathers so I won't drown)

AUDIENCE: *Kanyangali ya kanyangali*

NARRATOR: *Kanyangali nyangali nyangali* (Let me hold on to the feathers so I won't drown)

AUDIENCE: *Kanyangali ya kanyangali*

The big bird flapped its wing—flap! flap! flap!—until it reached the other side of the big river. The big bird returned two more times,

and each time the children sang the song until they reached the middle and most dangerous part of the river. The big bird finally returned for the last time to pick up the naughty child. The child was scared, and he cried because he was all by himself. All his sisters and brothers were gone. They were laughing and playing on the other side of the river. The bird picked up the child and told him to hold on tight to her big feathers. The bird began to fly. As soon as she began crossing the river, the child began to sing:

NARRATOR: *Kanyangali nyangali nyangali* (Let me hold on to the feathers so I won't drown)

AUDIENCE: *Kanyangali ya kanyangali*

NARRATOR: *Kanyangali nyangali nyangali* (Let me hold on to the feathers so I won't drown)

AUDIENCE: *Kanyangali ya kanyangali*

As the child held on to the feathers, they began to come off. The bird told him to hold on tight. The feathers were coming out. The child sang:

NARRATOR: *Kanyangali nyangali nyangali* (Let me hold on to the feathers so I won't drown)

AUDIENCE: *Kanyangali ya kanyangali*

NARRATOR: *Kanyangali nyangali nyangali* (Let me hold on to the feathers so I won't drown)

AUDIENCE: *Kanyangali ya kanyangali*

When they reached the very middle and the deepest part of the big river, the child lost his grip with his right claw as the feathers came out. He was now precariously hanging on by his left claw. The big bird told him to hold on tight and that his sisters and brothers were waiting for him on the other side. The child sang again:

NARRATOR: *Kanyangali nyangali nyangali* (Let me hold on to the feathers so I won't drown)

AUDIENCE: *Kanyangali ya kanyangali*

NARRATOR: *Kanyangali nyangali nyangali* (Let me hold on to the feathers so I won't drown)

AUDIENCE: *Kanyangali ya kanyangali*

The bird flew and flapped and flapped and flapped. The feathers that the child was holding on to with his left hand fell out. He fell into the raging water and drowned. The tale ends there. This tale teaches us not to disobey or insult our parents and others even though they may be crippled or have some other disability, for tomorrow we may meet with misfortune.

THE GIRL WHO DID NOT LISTEN

A long, long time ago, there were a man and a woman who were married. They had one child, whose name was Ngoza. One day they sent their daughter to the field to dig for peanuts. The parents told her that as she dug the peanuts, she would find some *mandolo*. (*Mandolo* are underdeveloped peanuts. The fresh, tender parts of these peanuts are very sweet. They are normally eaten fresh as people dig for peanuts in the field.) The parents knew that evil forces lurked in and haunted that part of the land, and they gave Ngoza strict instructions not to eat the mandolo. She was just to dig the peanuts. As the girl was digging, she indeed found the mandolo. She was very hungry. She succumbed to temptation and ate the mandolo, disobeying her parents.

When it was late in the afternoon, Ngoza wanted to return home to the village. Each time she tried to walk home, she failed. She tried again and again, failing each time. When darkness fell, her mother found Ngoza stuck in the field. Since she could not return home to the village, her father built her a house in the field. The parents had to bring food and feed her every day. Since it was dangerous in the bush, Ngoza had to be careful for whom she opened the door of the house. Her parents instructed her that she should open the door

Women have the responsibility of foraging for food. Here, a San (Bushman) woman searches for food in Botswana.

In many religious ceremonies, Africans will use traditional drums and other percussion instruments, including cowbells. Here, a tribe plays music during a religious ceremony in Ghana. Traditional drums are played only with sticks.

only if she heard "*Ngoza njulile.*" That would be the signal that her parents wanted to come in. Otherwise she should not open the door. Ngoza agreed.

Her mother went home and cooked nshima. She brought it back to the house in the field and sang:

> NARRATOR: *Ngoza njulile* (Ngoza, open for me)
>
> AUDIENCE: *Kaindeinde inde tate kainde*
>
> NARRATOR: *Ngoza njulile* (Ngoza, open for me)

AUDIENCE: *Kaindeinde inde tate kainde*

NARRATOR: *Ndine nyoko* (I am your mother)

AUDIENCE: *Kaindeinde inde tate kainde*

NARRATOR: *Ngoza njulile* (Ngoza, open for me)

AUDIENCE: *Kaindeinde inde tate kainde*

Ngoza opened the door. Her mother fed her and went home. The next time the mother came with food, she sang the same

NARRATOR: *Ngoza njulile* (Ngoza, open for me)

AUDIENCE: *Kaindeinde inde tate kainde*

NARRATOR: *Ndine nyoko* (I am your mother)

AUDIENCE: *Kaindeinde inde tate kainde*

NARRATOR: *Ngoza njulile* (Ngoza, open for me)

AUDIENCE: *Kaindeinde inde tate kainde*

Ngoza opened the door for her mother, who had brought some food. But this time, after Ngoza's mother left, the Hyena came to the house and sang:

NARRATOR: *Ngoza njulile* (Ngoza, open for me)

AUDIENCE: *Kaindeinde inde tate kainde*

NARRATOR: *Ngoza njulile* (Ngoza, open for me)

AUDIENCE: *Kaindeinde inde tate kainde*

NARRATOR: *Ndine mkwacha* (I am Mkwacha)

AUDIENCE: *Kaindeinde inde tate kainde*

NARRATOR: *Ngoza njulile* (Ngoza, open for me)

AUDIENCE: *Kaindeinde inde tate kainde*

The Hyena did not dance, let alone with mangwanda. However, Ngoza disobeyed her mother's strict instructions and opened the door. The Hyena ate her and then waited inside the house. Ngoza's mother came, danced with mangwanda, and sang the song:

NARRATOR: *Ngoza njulile* (Ngoza, open for me)

AUDIENCE: *Kaindeinde inde tate kainde*

NARRATOR: *Ngoza njulile* (Ngoza, open for me)

song and Ngoza opened the door. Before she left, her mother gave her new instructions. Next time, Ngoza should open the door only if she heard the song accompanied by dancing with *mangwanda* (rattles). Her mother went and bought some mangwanda to wear whenever she took food to her daughter. When she visited her daughter, dancing with mangwanda, Ngoza's mother sang:

NARRATOR: *Ngoza njulile* (Ngoza, open for me)

AUDIENCE: *Kaindeinde inde tate kainde*

This high-relief wood carving depicts a man wielding an axe and a machete, another man with an animal, and another drumming.

AUDIENCE: *Kaindeinde inde tate kainde*

NARRATOR: *Ndine nyoko* (I am your mother)

AUDIENCE: *Kaindeinde inde tate kainde*

NARRATOR: *Ngoza njulile* (Ngoza, open for me)

AUDIENCE: *Kaindeinde inde tate kainde*

The Hyena opened the door and ate Ngoza's mother. Later, Ngoza's father realized that his wife had not come back from taking food to their daughter. He went to the house in the field, carrying an axe. He sang the song:

NARRATOR: *Ngoza njulile* (Ngoza, open for me)

AUDIENCE: *Kaindeinde inde tate kainde*

NARRATOR: *Ngoza njulile* (Ngoza, open for me)

AUDIENCE: *Kaindeinde inde tate kainde*

NARRATOR: *Ndine wuso* (I am your father)

AUDIENCE: *Kaindeinde inde tate kainde*

NARRATOR: *Ngoza njulile* (Ngoza, open for me)

AUDIENCE: *Kaindeinde inde tate kainde*

The Hyena opened the door and Ngoza's father killed him with the axe. This is the end of the tale.

THE BIRD
AND THE HYENA

A long, long time ago, there was a king of all the villages in the land who could get everything he wanted. He had many wives. He had so much food that all he had to do was send his servants at any time day or night to bring him peanuts, beans, maize, and even meat. But the King was still unhappy because in all the land no one could bring him fish.

One day, he called all the people from the villages to gather at his palace. He said that anyone who could bring him fish could marry his beautiful daughter, the Princess. All the men tried but failed to bring fish. The king decided to send the Bird and the Hyena to bring

him fish. The two were to try to catch and bring him fish from a lake far, far away. The Bird traveled by day and the Hyena by night. As he traveled the Bird sang:

NARRATOR: *Ko ko*

AUDIENCE: *Kwenda kwamdinga linga*

NARRATOR: *Ko*

AUDIENCE: *Kwenda kwamdinga linga*

NARRATOR: *Afumu batituma*
   (The King has sent us)

AUDIENCE: *Kwenda kwamdinga linga*

NARRATOR: *Ko*

AUDIENCE: *Kwenda kwamdinga linga*

NARRATOR: *Somba ya mnyanja*
   (To get lake fish)

AUDIENCE: *Kwenda kwamdinga linga*

NARRATOR: *Ko*

Village life, the homestead, and polygamy among the Somburu of Kenya.

Inland lakes are often the only sources of fish and water for humans, birds, and animals in Africa. This is Lake Nakuru in the East African country of Kenya.

AUDIENCE: *Kwenda kwamdinga linga*

At the end of the day, the Bird stopped to sleep for the night. The Hyena started walking just after dark. He sang this song as he walked:

NARRATOR: *Huwi Huwi Huwi*

AUDIENCE: *Kwacha tikaone nyanja kwacha* (At daybreak we'll see the lake, at daybreak)

NARRATOR: *Huwi Huwi Huwi*

AUDIENCE: *Kwacha tikaone nyanja kwacha* (At daybreak we'll see the lake, at daybreak)

NARRATOR: *Huwi Huwi Huwi*

AUDIENCE: *Kwacha tikaone nyanja kwacha* (At daybreak we'll see the lake, at daybreak)

At daybreak, the Hyena stopped to sleep during the day. The Bird woke up to continue his journey. He sang his song. They traveled for many days and nights in this way. The Bird arrived at the big lake first. He caught as many fish as he could carry and dried them on the sand. The Hyena arrived the following day at daybreak. He also caught as many fish as he could carry and dried them on the sand. The following day, the Bird put his dry fish in a bag and set off on the long return journey. He sang:

NARRATOR: *Ko ko*

AUDIENCE: *Kwenda kwamdinga linga*

NARRATOR: *Ko*

AUDIENCE: *Kwenda kwamdinga linga*

NARRATOR: *Afumu batituma*
(The King has sent us)

AUDIENCE: *Kwenda kwamdinga linga*

NARRATOR: *Ko*

AUDIENCE: *Kwenda kwamdinga linga*

NARRATOR: *Somba ya mnyanja*
(To get lake fish)

AUDIENCE: *Kwenda kwamdinga linga*

NARRATOR: *Ko*

AUDIENCE: *Kwenda kwamdinga linga*

BELOW: In many parts of Africa the hyena has the reputation of being a filthy, sly nocturnal scavenger that makes devilish laughs in the middle of the pitch-dark African night. In most parts of rural Zambia, hyenas are associated with witches, since it is believed that witches ride them for long distances at night when they go to perform their evil deeds.

The following evening, the Hyena put his dry fish in a bag and set off on the long return journey. He sang:

NARRATOR: *Huwi Huwi Huwi*

AUDIENCE: *Kwacha tikaone nyanja kwacha* (At daybreak we'll see the lake, at daybreak)

NARRATOR: *Huwi Huwi Huwi*

AUDIENCE: *Kwacha tikaone nyanja kwacha* (At daybreak we'll see the lake, at daybreak)

NARRATOR: *Huwi Huwi Huwi*

AUDIENCE: *Kwacha tikaone nyanja kwacha* (At daybreak we'll see the lake, at daybreak)

A fertility staff from the Yoruba people of Nigeria. Some masks are used as fertility fetishes.

During the day the Bird flew and flew. At night the Hyena walked and walked. They both sang their songs many times until they arrived back at the village.

NARRATOR: *Ko ko*

AUDIENCE: *Kwenda kwamdinga linga*

NARRATOR: *Ko*

AUDIENCE: *Kwenda kwamdinga linga*

NARRATOR: *Afumu batituma* (The King has sent us)

AUDIENCE: *Kwenda kwamdinga linga*

NARRATOR: *Ko*

AUDIENCE: *Kwenda kwamdinga linga*

NARRATOR: *Somba ya mnyanja* (To get lake fish)

AUDIENCE: *Kwenda kwamdinga linga*

NARRATOR: *Ko*

AUDIENCE: *Kwenda kwamdinga linga*

The Bird was first to arrive. He gave the bag of dry fish to the King. Meanwhile, the Hyena was still on the road and sang:

NARRATOR: *Huwi Huwi Huwi*

AUDIENCE: *Kwacha tikaone nyanja kwacha* (At daybreak we'll see the lake, at daybreak)

NARRATOR: *Huwi Huwi Huwi*

AUDIENCE: *Kwacha tikaone nyanja kwacha* (At daybreak we'll see the lake, at daybreak)

NARRATOR: *Huwi Huwi Huwi*

AUDIENCE: *Kwacha tikaone nyanja kwacha* (At daybreak we'll see the lake, at daybreak)

The Hyena arrived in the village soon after that, but he was so hungry and greedy that he succumbed to temptation. He ate some of the fish before taking the rest to the King. The King said, "You, Hyena, have failed because you ate some of the fish before bringing it to me. Your reward is the fish that you have already eaten." The Bird married the Princess and lived happily ever after.

Boys go fishing and hunt small birds and animals, including mice, as rites of passage to manhood and to contribute to family meals. Young boys from shanty compounds and other areas on the outskirts of the city of Lusaka often hunt for mice. The mice are a delicacy and are used for family meals; the surplus is sold in the market.

THE DOG AND THE MBEBA HUNTERS

A long, long time ago, three boys set off from their village to hunt for *mbeba* (wild mice, a common delicacy among most peoples of Malawi, Zambia, and parts of Mozambique). The boys dug and dug for mbeba, but did not catch any. Meanwhile, the King's son, who was a good hunter, had also been hunting for mice that day. He had killed many of them and was returning home. The three boys, seeing the King's son carrying all the delicious mbeba, killed him and stole his mbeba. But what the boys did not know is that the King's son had been hunting with a small dog. This dog had seen everything. Hiding behind some bushes, the little dog began to follow the three boys as they walked back to the village. The little dog began to sing this song:

> **NARRATOR:** *Nke nke nke garu nke nke nke*
>
> **AUDIENCE:** *Garu* (Dog)

NARRATOR: *Nke nke nke garu nke nke nke*

AUDIENCE: *Garu* (Dog)

NARRATOR: *Bana aba* (These children)

AUDIENCE: *Garu* (Dog)

NARRATOR: *Bacekana* (They have cut each other)

AUDIENCE: *Garu* (Dog)

NARRATOR: *Pamutima* (On the heart)

AUDIENCE: *Garu* (Dog)

NARRATOR: *Tione wanune* (Let's see who is the most clever)

AUDIENCE: *Garu* (Dog)

NARRATOR: *Wanena ni uyu* (He is the one who said it)

AUDIENCE: *Garu* (Dog)

NARRATOR: *Nimwana wa fumu* (He is the King's son)

AUDIENCE: *Garu* (Dog)

NARRATOR: *Kancirikiti kumanda adapite na yani* (Who will go to the grave with them)

AUDIENCE: *Garu* (Dog)

NARRATOR: *Kancirikiti kumanda adapite na yani* (Who will go to the grave with them)

AUDIENCE: *Garu* (Dog)

Hearing the song, the boys tried to beat the dog and chased it many times. But the little dog eluded them, then continued to follow them and sing:

NARRATOR: *Nke nke nke garu nke nke nke*

AUDIENCE: *Garu* (Dog)

NARRATOR: *Nke nke nke garu nke nke nke*

AUDIENCE: *Garu* (Dog)

NARRATOR: *Bana aba* (These children)

AUDIENCE: *Garu* (Dog)

NARRATOR: *Bacekana* (They have cut each other)

AUDIENCE: *Garu* (Dog)

NARRATOR: *Pamutima* (On the heart)

AUDIENCE: *Garu* (Dog)

NARRATOR: *Tione wanune* (Let's see who is the most clever)

AUDIENCE: *Garu* (Dog)

NARRATOR: *Wanena ni uyu* (He is the one who said it)

AUDIENCE: *Garu* (Dog)

NARRATOR: *Nimwana wa fumu* (He is the King's son)

AUDIENCE: *Garu* (Dog)

NARRATOR: *Kancirikiti kumanda adapite na yani* (Who will go to the grave with them)

AUDIENCE: *Garu* (Dog)

NARRATOR: *Kancirikiti kumanda adapite na yani* (Who will go to the grave with them)

AUDIENCE: *Garu* (Dog)

When they arrived back at the village, the little dog sat down by the mortar where the women were pounding corn. The little dog sang the song again:

NARRATOR: *Nke nke nke garu nke nke nke*

AUDIENCE: *Garu* (Dog)

NARRATOR: *Nke nke nke garu nke nke nke*

AUDIENCE: *Garu* (Dog)

NARRATOR: *Bana aba* (These children)

Women spend hours pounding corn into cornmeal, which they use for cooking meals for their families in all the villages of Zambia. This domestic work is also performed communally as these women help each other in pounding the same corn together.

Ritual painting of the body is a common practice in many traditional African initiation rights. These are Pondo tribe children at Grahamstown in the Cape Province in South Africa.

AUDIENCE: *Garu* (Dog)

NARRATOR: *Bacekana*
(They have cut each other)

AUDIENCE: *Garu* (Dog)

NARRATOR: *Pamutima*
(On the heart)

AUDIENCE: *Garu* (Dog)

NARRATOR: *Tione wanune* (Let's see who is the most clever)

AUDIENCE: *Garu* (Dog)

NARRATOR: *Wanena ni uyu*
(He is the one who said it)

AUDIENCE: *Garu* (Dog)

NARRATOR: *Nimwana wa fumu*
(He is the King's son)

AUDIENCE: *Garu* (Dog)

NARRATOR: *Kancirikiti kumanda adapite na yani* (Who will go to the grave with them)

AUDIENCE: *Garu* (Dog)

NARRATOR: *Kancirikiti kumanda adapite na yani* (Who will go to the grave with them)

AUDIENCE: *Garu* (Dog)

During wedding ceremonies, there is celebration and dancing. These women are dancing at a wedding ceremony in Senegal.

The women heard the song and asked the boys what it all meant. The boys confessed that they had killed the King's son and stolen his mbeba.

A WOMAN AND THE MONKEY

This folktale is very contemporary as it incorporates many ideas and items of the modern consumer culture.

A long, long time ago, there was a beautiful young woman in a village. Many men came to the village *nthanganeni*. (A *nthanganeni* is a hut in the village in which single young women and girls sleep. The young women work, eat, and interact with their families during the day, but at night they all sleep in the one hut. Any potential suitors go to the nthanganeni in order to propose marriage and court the young women they are attracted to.) Each of the men proposed marriage to the young woman, but she was too proud and rejected them all. She said they were neither handsome nor good enough for her.

One day a monkey put on a very good suit, shoes, and tie and came to the nthanganeni. He proposed marriage to the woman. The woman accepted the marriage proposal, saying that he was the handsome man she had been waiting for. A few months later they were married.

One afternoon, a few weeks after they had been married, the new bridegroom went to the river with his wife's younger brother to take a bath. The boy noticed that his new brother-in-law was taking a bath separately, in hiding. This happened every time they went to the river to take a bath.

"Brother-in-law, why do you always take a bath away from me?" the boy asked. "I never see you naked."

"Well," the brother-in-law replied, "I really cannot take a bath with you since you are...well...I am a shy man."

One day the boy decided to hide behind bushes on the riverbank to observe his secretive brother-in-law take a bath and watched him undress. Once his brother-in-law was naked, the boy came out of the bushes.

"Brother-in-law," the boy said, "I can see that you have a very dark mouth and lips. Why?"

"Well," replied the monkey, "it is because I drink lots of hot tea." He sang this song:

NARRATOR: *Ni tiyi uyu* (This is tea)

AUDIENCE: *Keke wangondola keke*
(Cake, I used to eat cake)

NARRATOR: *Tika umwanga*
(We used to drink it)

AUDIENCE: *Keke wangondola keke*
(Cake, I used to eat cake)

NARRATOR: *Ku regimenti*
(In the army regiment)

AUDIENCE: *Keke wangondola keke*
(Cake, I used to eat cake)

NARRATOR: *Keke mulamu*
(Cake, brother-in-law)

AUDIENCE: *Keke wangondola keke*
(Cake, I used to eat cake)

NARRATOR: *Keke mulamu*
(Cake, brother-in-law)

AUDIENCE: *Keke wangondola keke*
(Cake, I used to eat cake)

A male fetish figure with nails and mirrors. This fetish is used to achieve desired goals through magical actions among the Bakongo.

The boy then noticed *vimphata* (red patches on the monkey's bottom) and asked his brother-in-law what that was. He replied that it was his pair of trousers.

NARRATOR: *Buluku ili*
(These trousers)

AUDIENCE: *Keke wangondola keke*
(Cake, I used to eat cake)

NARRATOR: *Tikabvwalanga*
(I used to wear them)

AUDIENCE: *Keke wangondola keke*
(Cake, I used to eat cake)

NARRATOR: *Ku regimenti*
(In the army regiment)

AUDIENCE: *Keke wangondola keke*
(Cake, I used to eat cake)

NARRATOR: *Keke mulamu*
(Cake, brother-in-law)

AUDIENCE: *Keke wangondola keke*
(Cake, I used to eat cake)

NARRATOR: *Keke mulamu*
(Cake, brother-in-law)

AUDIENCE: *Keke wangondola keke*
(Cake, I used to eat cake)

The boy noticed that his brother-in-law had eyes that were sunk very deep in his sockets. When the boy asked why his eyes were that way, the monkey replied that it was because he used to wear eyeglasses.

NARRATOR: *Magalasi aba*
(These eyeglasses)

AUDIENCE: *Keke wangondola keke*
(Cake, I used to eat cake)

NARRATOR: *Tikabvwalanga*
(I used to wear them)

AUDIENCE: *Keke wangondola keke*
(Cake, I used to eat cake)

NARRATOR: *Ku regimenti*
(In the army regiment)

AUDIENCE: *Keke wangondola keke*
(Cake, I used to eat cake)

NARRATOR: *Keke mulamu*
(Cake, brother-in-law)

AUDIENCE: *Keke wangondola keke*
    (Cake, I used to eat cake)

NARRATOR: *Keke mulamu*
    (Cake, brother-in-law)

AUDIENCE: *Keke wangondola keke*
    (Cake, I used to eat cake)

The boy noticed that his brother-in-law's feet had long toes. He asked him why his toes were that way. The monkey answered that it was from wearing shoes.

NARRATOR: *Skapato izi*
    (These shoes)

AUDIENCE: *Keke wangondola keke*
    (Cake, I used to eat cake)

NARRATOR: *Tikabvwalanga*
    (I used to wear them)

AUDIENCE: *Keke wangondola keke*
    (Cake, I used to eat cake)

NARRATOR: *Ku regimenti*
    (In the army regiment)

AUDIENCE: *Keke wangondola keke*
    (Cake, I used to eat cake)

NARRATOR: *Keke mulamu*
    (Cake, brother-in-law)

AUDIENCE: *Keke wangondola keke*
    (Cake, I used to eat cake)

NARRATOR: *Keke mulamu*
    (Cake, brother-in-law)

AUDIENCE: *Keke wangondola keke*
    (Cake, I used to eat cake)

The boy noticed that his brother-in-law had very long sharp teeth. He asked him about them. The monkey answered that it was because he used to eat a lot of bread.

NARRATOR: *Buledi ili* (This bread)

AUDIENCE: *Keke wangondola keke*
    (Cake, I used to eat cake)

NARRATOR: *Tikajemulanga*
    (I used to take big bites)

AUDIENCE: *Keke wangondola keke*
    (Cake, I used to eat cake)

NARRATOR: *Ku regimenti*
    (In the army regiment)

AUDIENCE: *Keke wangondola keke*
    (Cake, I used to eat cake)

NARRATOR: *Keke mulamu*
    (Cake, brother-in-law)

AUDIENCE: *Keke wangondola keke*
    (Cake, I used to eat cake)

NARRATOR: *Keke mulamu*
    (Cake, brother-in-law)

AUDIENCE: *Keke wangondola keke*
    (Cake, I used to eat cake)

The boy ran to the village as fast as he could. He asked his older sister to come and see her new husband at the river. When they arrived at the river, she was shocked to find that her husband was actually a monkey. He had fooled her by wearing nice clothes. She told him that their marriage was over. The monkey was so ashamed to be discovered that he ran away into the bush.

Physical environments that can support a wide variety of wildlife are very quickly dwindling in Africa. These lions are resting in an area that may fall victim to expanding population and pressures for arable land.

KALULU
THE HARE AND
THE LION

A long, long time ago, Kalulu the Hare was walking along the road in search of a job when he saw the Lion.

"King," Kalulu said to the lion, "I am looking for a job."

"I have a job for you, Kalulu," replied the Lion. "Would you look after my children when I go hunting?"

"Yes, King," answered Kalulu. "I do like to play with children. I will take the job."

So Kalulu started working for the Lion. He watched and played with her children. (In the Tumbuka language the pronouns "she" and "he" are rarely emphasized or used or are not a prominent aspect of the normal everyday language. As a result, "King" and "she" are always used interchangeably in storytelling. A male animal will have children. The modern reader could say that in this sense the Tumbuka and many Bantu languages are nonsexist.) The Lion went very far to hunt. She brought back home a lot of meat. She instructed Kalulu to cook the meat and feed the

children. The Lion went away again to hunt some more. Kalulu cooked all the meat. He took the fat or grease from the meat and smeared it around the children's lips. Kalulu ate all the meat himself. The Lion returned and heard her children crying.

"Kalulu, why are the children crying?" the Lion asked.

"King, they are hungry," replied Kalulu.

"Didn't they eat all that meat?"

"Yes, but it wasn't enough," replied Kalulu. "They are still hungry."

The Lion went very, very far away again to hunt some more. Kalulu felt hungry. He told two of the children to fight and that whoever fell down was going to be eaten. One of the children fell down, and Kalulu and the lion children ate him. He told the other children to fight. One of them fell down and was eaten. In the end only Kalulu and one of the Lion's children remained. The Lion suddenly returned.

"Kalulu, where are all the children?"

"Oh, King!" cried Kalulu. "Many monkeys came here and threatened to kill us. I ran away and hid with one of the children. The other children were killed and eaten by the monkeys."

The Lion was very angry. He asked Kalulu what he should do. Kalulu said he had a plan.

"King, I will tie you up in a big bundle of grass. I will go and call all the monkeys to come here and help me eat peanuts which are tied up in a big bundle of grass. You will then come out and punish all the monkeys."

The Lion agreed to the plan. Kalulu built a big fence out of grass and put the Lion inside a big bundle of grass that he had gathered. Kalulu set off yelling and calling all the monkeys. The other animals in the forest, including zebras, buffalo, antelopes, foxes, and tortoises, wondered what Kalulu was calling the monkeys for. All the monkeys eventually gathered.

"I have called all of you here," Kalulu yelled loudly, "because I am holding a very big banquet. You are all invited to come and eat peanuts with me. I have tied these peanuts in a big bundle of grass."

Kalulu told the monkeys that once they got to his house he would lead them in a song with these words:

> NARRATOR: *Ndani anapha bana bankharamu* (Who killed the Lion's children?)
>
> AUDIENCE: *Ndife ndife ndife* (It's us, it's us, it's us)
>
> NARRATOR: *Ndani anapha bana bankharamu* (Who killed the Lion's children?)
>
> NARRATOR: *Ndife ndife ndife* (It's us, it's us, it's us)

Kalulu walked with the monkeys to the entrance of the big fence. He told them that once they were inside, he was going to lock the door so that nobody would disturb them during the banquet. They were to sing the song. After they were finished singing, they were to tear up the big bundle of grass to get the delicious peanuts. The monkeys entered and Kalulu closed the door. The monkey sang the song:

> NARRATOR: *Ndani anapha bana bankharamu* (Who killed the Lion's children?)
>
> AUDIENCE: *Ndife ndife ndife* (It's us, it's us, it's us)
>
> NARRATOR: *Ndani anapha bana bankharamu* (Who killed the Lion's children?)
>
> AUDIENCE: *Ndife ndife ndife* (It's us, it's us, it's us)

The monkeys tore up the big bundle of grass. The Lion jumped out and killed all the monkeys. Kalulu ran away into the bush.

The expansion of road networks provides quick and comfortable transportation for both vehicles and pedestrians in many parts of rural Africa, but this development is also reducing environments that can support wildlife. Women carrying and balancing goods on their heads, holding a baby, and walking along the roads with their children are a common sight.

TRADITIONAL AND CONTEMPORARY LEGENDS

Every African tribe has legends about the founders and heroes of the group that illustrate thought and religion, history and prehistory. In this aspect, myths and legends tend to overlap. Nevertheless, while a myth may narrate a story about the supernatural or about the origin of an African people, legends are traditional stories that tell of historical occurrences relating to significant events in the more recent lives of Africans. Geoffrey Parrinder says, "A myth is a story of supernatural or primeval beings which cannot be placed

A bronze sculpture known as the
Altar of the Hand from Benin
in West Africa.

ABOVE: This magnificent royal state stool carved out of wood and decorated with silver belonged to an *asantehene* (Ashanti ruler) of the nineteenth century in Ghana in West Africa. The circular part of the wooden object depicts the proverb "The rainbow is around the neck of every nation," which refers to the king's responsibility in uniting the different Asante chiefdoms. According to legend, the stool was removed from the Asantehene's palace at Kumasi in November 1873.

RIGHT: Professional carvers make wooden stools to order among the Ashanti people near the town of Kumasi in Ghana.

in recorded history. A legend is a traditional story, about historical or semi-historical people, even if the narratives are partly imaginary, and many stories include both myth and legend."

This overlap between myths and legends is illustrated in a number of legends from several parts of Africa. For example, the significance of the ceremonial stool that belongs to

the Ashanti King in Ghana in West Africa goes back to the fourth king of the Ashanti in the eighteenth century. According to the legend, the Ashanti were an ordinary people until their king, Osai Tutu, made them into a great nation. The story is that an ordinary clansman, Anotchi, lived in a neighboring kingdom. He was so well versed in medicine and magic that when he fled to the Ashanti, he said that Nyame, the Supreme God, had sent him to make the Ashanti a great people. Anotchi went to Osai Tutu and, using his spiritual powers, summoned a thundering black cloud from which emerged a wooden stool covered with gold. Anotchi told the Ashanti King and his people that the Golden Stool would be responsible for their welfare and good health.

This is said to be how the Ashanti ceremonial stool came into being. Through wars with neighboring states and British colonial conquest, the Golden Stool has remained a sacred and revered centerpiece of the Ashanti monarchy. The ceremonial stool still exists today among the Ashanti. The overlap between myth and legend is evident because the origin of the Ashanti in connection with the stool

has many mythical qualities. Anotchi used his spiritual powers to conjure a black cloud out of which the Golden Stool appeared. The Golden Stool contained the soul of the Ashanti people, and legend has it that the stool was symbolic motivation for the Ashanti during their resistance against British colonialism during the late 1800s.

Another legend relates to the spectacular art found at Ife in Nigeria, which includes bronzes that date back to the thirteenth and fourteenth centuries. In Yoruban creation mythology, Ile-Ife, or "the house of Ife," is regarded as the place of origin. It is said that the Supreme God (the King of Ife) had several sons. Benin mythology says that the youngest son of the Supreme God founded the Kingdom of Benin. The legend states that the very first people of Benin could not agree on anything and thus did not have a ruler. Eventually, they sent a message to the King of Ife asking him to send one of his sons to rule them. This son brought the snail shell containing the earth. When the earth fell out of it and covered the marsh, the son was given authority over Benin. The actual shell is believed to be one found in Nigeria and made

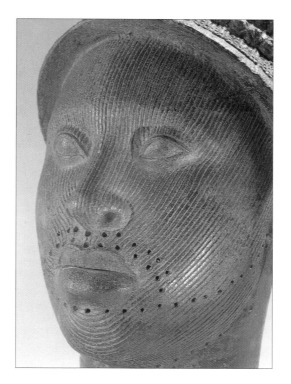

out of brass. It is now preserved in the royal palace. This is how the craftsmanship of Ife was passed on to the Kingdom of Benin.

The Gikuyu people of Kenya have myths and legends about their creation. They say that in the beginning, the creator, God, made a great mountain as a sign of his prowess. This is known as Kere Nyanga, which Europeans call Mount Kenya.

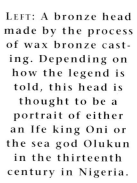

LEFT: A bronze head made by the process of wax bronze casting. Depending on how the legend is told, this head is thought to be a portrait of either an Ife king Oni or the sea god Olukun in the thirteenth century in Nigeria.

BELOW: Mount Kenya, also known throughout the world as Mount Kirinyaga.

ABOVE: Some wooden figurines are carved to depict powerful magical forces. This witchcraft figure from the Chokwe people of the Northwestern Province of Zambia is on display in the Livingstone Museum.

RIGHT: A knife handle from the Yoruba people of Nigeria.

One version of the myth says that God gave a choice of tools to his three sons who were the fathers of the Kikuyu, Masai, and Kamba tribes of Kenya. They had to choose between a spear, a bow, and a digging stick. The father of the Kikuyu people chose the digging stick and this how they became farmers.

Another version of the myth says that in the middle of the country where there were clusters of trees, God told Gikuyu to make a home. God gave him a wife called Moombi, who bore him nine daughters. Gikuyu, however, was unhappy about not having sons. He went to the mountain and called on God. God told Gikuyu to follow special instructions in making sacrifice. Afterward, Gikuyu found nine young men under a fig tree. They married his nine daughters and willingly agreed to live in a matriarchal, or female-dominated, family. The nine daughters are the ancestors of the nine Chief Kikuyu clans and the whole tribe of Moombi.

ANIMAL
LEGENDS

Animals have always been an integral part of traditional African life. Since villages were located in the middle of the wilderness, until recently Africans did not have a sharp physical or mental separation between themselves and wild animals.

Animals were often a source of nourishment as well as danger. Some animals served as a source of inspiration due to their sheer cunning, strength, and endurance. For example, among the people of the Eastern Province of Zambia, wild dogs are believed to be so tenacious that they will chase an animal and eat it as it runs. By the time the large prey falls, half of it will already have been eaten. The leopard is also believed to be a very tenacious animal that does not die easily. The brute strength and pride of the lion is well recognized all over the world and induces fear in man. The hare is believed to be swift and cunning. According to Naboth Ngulube, in his book *Growing Up in Zambia*, the hyena is believed to be devious and evil, and is associated with witchcraft. Ngulube says, "The hyena is actually the horse for the witch. It is virtually impossible for traditional hunters to kill a hyena. A hyena killed anywhere amongst villages creates unprecedented curiosity and stories of how the owners mourned for the hyenas. The owners in this case are witches." This was the period during African history when wild animals were plentiful, men coexisted with them, and there was no sharp separation between where men and animals lived. This inspired a distinctive cultural integration of wild animals into African lives. For example, many African societies used animals as a means of clan identification. This is known as totemism. Members who identified themselves with the animal totemic symbol would not harm or eat that animal, believing that such behavior would harm the clan.

One of the consequences of European colonialism is that the West introduced monotheism combined with capitalism. The notion that there is a hierarchy of one supreme god, humans, and then animals has since gained ground in Africa. Thus, Africans have become physically and mentally separated from wild animals and have come to see them as a means of earning money. The concept of the game reserve is a strictly Western idea that has been implemented in Africa and has caused a serious conflict between humans' interests and the objective of animal and wildlife conservation. Before European colonization, Africans used bows and arrows to kill wild animals for consumption or if a particular animal endangered their lives. Now, many Africans kill animals in large numbers using modern weapons for commercial gain. For example, until the recent worldwide ban, elephants were killed for their ivory, which fetched very good money. Today, many Africans still poach buffalo, hippopotami, impala, and other wild game to sell for money. This has transformed the fundamental attitude of Africans toward animals. Animals now may be regarded as just another commodity that can be sold. Killing animals in large numbers for profit is a capitalistic Western concept. Thirty to fifty years ago, humans and animals coexisted; this coexistence spawned many legends and myths.

As the human population has increased and the technology of hunting has become more efficient in Africa, many animal populations have dwindled and are now mainly confined to game parks. In spite of exotic images about wild Africa that still prevail in the Western media today, the reality is that wild animals are so few that the vast majority of the more than 680 million Africans will not see many of these wild animals in their entire lives. This is perhaps why the animal legends and myths that follow, which may not have been documented by Europeans, are of even more importance as they reflect the awe, inspiration, and sometimes utter bewilderment that animals once caused in the lives of Africans.

Before the African population increased and Westernization changed the relationship between humans and wild animals, I was fortunate to experience the last of the truly wild Africa in the late 1950s as a young child liv-

ing with my parents in the Luangwa Valley of Eastern Zambia among the Bisa people. One true story will illustrate how closely Africans lived with wild animals.

One day, my father was gone for a few days on a business trip. I was about seven years old. My mother told me to sleep in my father's bed instead of in my room. My mother slept with my ten-month-old baby sister. It was around seven in the evening and my sister was whining and being naughty. Suddenly, two lions alternately roared barely ten yards (9m) from the bedroom window. My mother quickly blew out the kerosene lamp. Pots and pans crashed to the floor and rats

Ancient rock paintings in caves often depict the animals that ancient Africans hunted in the open savannah grassland and are still common in Africa.

dropped from the grass roof. The whole house vibrated. I froze and could not even pull the covers over my head to hide. There was commotion and screaming in the nearby village. After what seemed like an eternity of alternate roaring, the lions seemed to walk away. My mother and I did not get out of bed until morning because my mother thought the lions might have been still waiting for us outside. My mother prayed, thanking God for saving our lives. As a young child, the experience made a great impression on me.

Many experiences involving wild animals in the valley and elsewhere in Africa ended in tragedy, however. That was part of living in undeveloped Africa. The myths and legends that this closeness to wild animals inspired are many and varied, but only a few will be described here.

One day at Chasela Primary School, it was discovered that a student was missing. It turned out that the student had been caught by a leopard while walking to school through grasses that grew tall during the rainy season. Children were instructed to walk to school in groups of five or six. However, even a small group would not deter a man-eating leopard.

It was believed that once a wild animal had eaten human flesh, it would eat nothing else. Word was sent to Fort Jameson (now Chipata) to have the British colonial district commissioner send some game wardens to hunt down the man-eating leopard. By this time the villages were in a state of siege, as five children had been killed and eaten, and a sixth child was missing.

The European wardens arrived, and after they had located the remains of the sixth child in a tree, they set up a trap. They knew that a leopard always comes back to where it has left some of its kill to eat later. At dusk the wardens set up their Jeep facing the low-hanging branches of the tree, and sat and waited with their loaded shotguns. After a long wait in the dark, the wardens heard the trees rustling. They switched on the bright headlamps of the Jeep. The leopard was back. Caught dead in the middle of the glare, it wagged its tail and then froze momentarily. The wardens shot the leopard once, but it still stood as if ready to pounce. The leopard was so tenacious that when they fired the ninth round, it still charged at the wardens before it finally collapsed dead.

Many Africans derive their traditional dances from the behavior and movements of both domestic and wild animals. These men of the San (Bushmen) of the Kalahari Desert are doing the ostrich dance.

Among the Bisa, there is a story of a man who was walking with his son to the fields. Suddenly a lone angry buffalo charged at him from behind the thick rainy-season bushes. The man accidentally dropped his spear. Since he could not retrieve his spear, he grabbed the buffalo by the horns. He yelled to his son to get the spear and stab the animal from behind. The son speared the animal through its anus and twisted the spear as many times as possible. After a brief struggle, the buffalo collapsed and died. They shared the meat with the rest of the village.

Although many legends are about large animals like buffalo, hyenas, and lions, there are equally as many, especially among the people of the Eastern Province of Zambia, that are about such animals as snakes and mice. To African people, snakes have a very terrifying reputation, for good reason. The majority of African snakes are poisonous, and a few of these are very deadly. The snake known as *sato* in the Eastern Province of Zambia can grow to more than twenty feet (6m) long. It is slow and is believed to suffocate prey as big as a buck before swallowing it whole. It will then sit in the same place until it sheds. Then it will move on to get its next prey. It is believed that some women use the sato's heart in love potions. A man who has been fed a sato's heart will not travel very far from his home. The man may be tempted by his friends to go out for a drink or other activity, but he will refuse to leave his home, finding an excuse to stay close to his wife. Thus, men who exhibit such behavior are said to have been fed the sato's heart by their wives.

An elderly man from the Lundazi district whom I interviewed in Lusaka in June 1976 told me about a snake that lived during the period between 1920 and 1940 and was called *bvwila*. This was a long, big, black snake. When it coiled itself, it made such a big heap that one could not see where it hid its head.

It lived in the distant, quiet environment of the rocky hills that were uninhabited by humans. However, if hunting parties came across it, they always wanted to kill it. Its mere breath could kill human beings in close vicinity, and those who were farther away would get sick.

The same species of snake is believed to have been killed in the city of Luanshya in the copper belt of Zambia during the colonial era. During those days, urban areas had their water supply pumped and passed through an open concrete gutter to the town reservoir. The bvwila snake in Luanshya used to cross through this water source, which was in its path. When this same water was drunk by Luanshya township residents, they died. Knowing the poisonous nature of its breath, the people tried to kill the snake without coming too close. They laid down sharp razors along its path. When the snake slithered across the razors, it split open and died.

According to the man I spoke to, in the olden days of Lundazi, the people had a very peculiar method of killing this very poisonous snake. When they located a hole in which the snake lived, similar to an anthill, they would build a small, igloolike structure of mud around the hill and then pass several very sharp spears through it. When the snake tried

A lone African Cape buffalo has the legendary reputation of being one of the meanest wild animals when angered. Even lions will not attack it from the front for fear of sustaining mortal injury.

to come out, it would struggle, cut itself against the spears in the process, and die. Through this method, many people were saved from its poisonous breath.

The bvwila's heart is believed to have been very much sought after, as it was used for charms and the treatment of certain diseases. The word *bvwila* means "to help" in Tumbuka. Its name could have been derived from the curative nature of certain of its biological organs. However, the primary reason for killing the snake every time it was found was because it was extraordinarily poisonous. Since then the snake is said to have been killed off until it became extinct.

A famous legend among the people of the Eastern Province of Zambia pits the *mbobo* snake against a group of boys, and shows what happens when one is careless. The significance of this legend cannot be appreciated unless one is familiar with the status of the mbobo snake in these people's folklore, the use of mice as a dietary supplement, and the prevalence of hunting mice among young boys. According to these people, the mbobo snake, or black mamba, is the deadliest snake known to man. Elders, often in a hushed, excited tone, describe how, when provoked, the mbobo can stand on its tail while chasing a man, thus increasing its speed.

Legends about animals are derived from men's experiences with hunting, as these men of the San (Bushmen) of the Kalahari Desert are doing.

Hunting in the wild for mice to eat is a very common activity among the Bantu peoples of Central Africa and parts of Southern Africa. Most rural people in Zambia's Eastern Province and parts of northern Malawi, an estimated population of more than one million, eat mice as a traditional delicacy. This is true of such tribes as the Tumbuka, Senga, Chewa, Ngoni, and Nsenga. All of these peoples have long agricultural traditions.

A common expression among the Tumbuka refers to a couple's yearning for a baby boy so that he can kill mice for them when he grows up. Parents chastise boys who bully their little sisters by asking them, "Who is go-

ing to cook mice for you when you grow up?" One of the traditional criteria for a boy's growing to manhood was the ability to dig for and kill mice. If a child is running and accidentally trips and falls, an adult will console him by dusting him off and saying, "Never mind, you killed a mouse."

Another famous tale illustrates how embedded the capture and eating of mice is in Tumbuka culture. A man went to the fields and caught six mice. He brought them home to the village for his wife to cook. She dried them nicely. The man ate two of them with nshima and enjoyed them a great deal. However, at the next meal, to the husband's chagrin, he was served the nshima meal with *delele* (a leafy vegetable). He angrily summoned his wife for an explanation. The husband stated that there had been six mice, but he had eaten only two. He asked where the other four had gone. The poor wife explained that she and the children had eaten two and her uncle and other guests who had visited earlier had eaten the others. The husband gave the wife a beating for being so irresponsible. The wife wailed, saying that her brute of a husband was killing her because of mice.

In the village court, the elders severely rebuked the husband. He was disgraced in his

Its sharp eyes and reflexes enable the deadly mbobo (black mouth mamba) snake to dodge even a fast-moving shot from a pellet gun aimed at its head.

Small paths often criss-cross the *dambo* plains connecting villages. This woman and her child return to the village by walking through a dambo near Oshikati in Namibia.

THE SNAKE AND THE MICE HUNTERS

This legend is a modified version from my article "The Dry Season and the Art of Digging and Eating Mbeba" in *Titbits for the Curious*. This part of the book includes an examination of the socialization of boys in hunting mice. My source of information was a man from the Chewa people in Chief Chikomeni in the Lundazi district of Eastern Zambia.

One morning, a young boy and his friends, deciding to satisfy their curiosity, smoked *dagga*, or cannabis. They hid in the bushes on the outskirts of the village, out of sight of adults. As the boy and the three friends were smoking, they noticed black smoke clouds high in the sky over the *dambo* (low-lying land which is often found at the sources of rivers and streams) where women from their village drew water.

He and his friends were excited about this because burnt grass made it easier to find mouse holes, dig, and chase the mice because all the obstructing bush was cleared. By the time they got a hoe to dig with and headed toward the burning dambo bush, they were feeling excited, giddy, and goofy. As they walked through the dambo's burnt ashes in search of a mouse hole, some of the dry grass and sticks were still smoldering. The fire was still burning the wild grass ahead of them. After a while, they located a mouse hole that looked promising.

Digging mice requires certain skills and knowledge. If the mouse hole is big, shallow, and parallel to the surface, the digger has to be cautious because then anything can be in it—stinging ants, frogs, poisonous spiders, rabbits, snakes, small and big blue-headed lizards, scorpions, and even porcupines. Although this hole was big and parallel to the surface, the boys threw caution to the wind. They joked, giggled, and laughed about what

village and the surrounding towns because he was trying to run what was going on in the kitchen and particularly the "kitchen pot," which was hardly a man's responsibility. From that time, the story tells us, men have never counted pieces of meat in the kitchen pot, be they beef, chicken, small birds, or eggs. The legend plays many functions among the Tumbuka. It defines limits of behavior between married men and women, reaffirms sexual division of labor and responsibilities, and discourages physical abuse of wives. The punishment for an erring husband will be public shame and disgrace.

they would find in the hole. One of the friends even teased that the other boy's grandfather (who was still living) would come out.

After digging for a short while, one boy exclaimed to the others that he could see the tail of a big mouse in the hole. Another boy, giggling, volunteered to catch the mouse at the escape hole. "Why should we bother ourselves chasing this lone mouse?" the boy asked. Of course this gesture was a joke as boys preferred to hit a mouse from a distance with a knobkerrie, or short stick, rather than trying to catch it in their hands. All the time this was happening, everyone was laughing and having a good time.

The boy crouched near the escape hole and placed his hand around it. His friends were also on guard just in case there was more than one mouse. They waited. The boy who was digging pushed a *mtokoso* into the hole. (A *mtokoso* is a short stick boys use when they are digging for mice. They shove it into the hole to see if that will force the mice to come out.) Everybody raised their sticks in readiness as he pushed further. The boy saw a small head emerging from the escape hole. As it pushed its head out, the boy quickly closed his right hand and fingers around its neck in a tight grip. This thing felt different in his hand—it was a snake, the feared mbobo, or black mamba.

The snake's eyes were bulging out and green with rage. Annoyed with the suffocating pressure around its neck, it struggled and coiled itself around the boy's arm. His friends fled for dear life. The women drawing water nearby dropped their water containers and ran away wailing. They noticed the boy's inescapable plight and dashed home to to the village to convey the message of his death to his parents.

At first the boy was stunned and frozen to the spot. Then he cried with terror, because he was alone, helpless and abandoned by his friends to face certain death. He felt power leave the rest of his body and accumulate in his right hand to help squeeze the creature's neck. His instinct was to squeeze it to death. But it did not die. Several times it coiled round his small short arm and he tried to fling it away but he still held firmly to its neck. All of this might have taken a few seconds, but the boy felt as if he had spent a few days in this agonizing emotional condition. The snake had not yet bitten him. He had to think fast. He felt his blood melt. For the last time, the boy summoned all the strength to his right hand. The snake coiled around his arm once again. With all his might, the boy hurled it about twenty yards (8m) away and fled in the opposite direction, homeward.

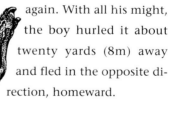

ABOVE: **Snakes have very important symbolic values in many African societies. Here is a Bakongo figurine of a woman with a drum and a snake.**

LEFT: **Pythons suffocate their prey to death. A South African species of rock python eats small prey, contrary to the legend that pythons can swallow a whole deer and, by implication, a grown human.**

The black mamba, the fastest and most poisonous African snake, recovered from its fall and, within seconds, was running after the boy at his tallest height, with half its body vertical to the ground. The boy was light and used to running but he could not outrun a black mamba, which is well known for its tremendous speed, particularly in bushes. However, all of the bushes on the dambo had been burnt away by the fire. It was a race between the two of them, and dust and ashes rose in their trail.

The boy had never run as fast as he did that day. He glanced back and there the snake was, gliding at an incredibly fast speed with its small head just above the boy's head, ready to strike him. The boy ducked to one side and made a sudden sharp turn. Staggering, he regained his balance and resumed running. At that speed, the snake could not make instant turns, so momentum carried it forward and it stopped about fifty yards (46m) away. By the time it turned around to resume its chase, the boy was forced to run in a different

Dambos are flat plains with short grass and pools of water from which humans get bathing water and domestic and wild animals get their drinking water. The available water can also be used in gardens.

direction, away from home, where there was little likelihood of being rescued. He avoided the snake's lethal strike twice in this manner.

The boy was now tired and worn out. He was ready to give up and resign himself to his fate. The last of his energy had been exhausted. He was hoping someone would save him. Perhaps more miracles would happen. The wretched snake was still after him.

Ahead of him there was a pond of water surrounded by thick vegetation of creeping plants. He was going to plunge into the water.

A Fang mask of the Ngontang society.

Maybe by sheer chance, the snake did not know how to swim. Just at the edge of the water, the boy slipped and fell flat on the mud. At full speed, the mbobo snake plunged into the pool of dark water. It would now come to finish him with its deadly fangs. The boy tried to rise, but his power was gone, he had no strength to command his body. He was stuck in the mud. Then the boy lost consciousness.

When the boy regained consciousness, he was in his father's house lying on a mat and surrounded by a lot of people from the village who were obviously in transition from misery to relief. Some were mourning. The boy started crying. Surely, the snake must have bitten him. Why wasn't he dead?

But later he learned that the snake did not return. Maybe the cool water calmed it after the giant race or maybe it had drowned. People had flocked to the dambo instantly on hearing the alarming news. They had picked up the unconscious boy on the edge of the pond. Expecting the worst, the boy's father had torn into the bush immediately with an axe clinging to his broad shoulders. He had brought a variety of herbs from the bush, some for dissipating frightening aftereffects, and some for treating snakebite. The boy took some of the herbs.

Normally, the boy slept with the other boys in the *mphala* (a hut where unmarried young men and boys sleep in the village). However, this night the boy slept with his two older sisters who had huge, heavy bosoms. Continuous hard work in the field had developed their arm muscles to a proportion similar to their menfolk. At night, the boy violently woke up with an ear-splitting scream. The huge, green-eyed, menacing black mamba was before his sight again. This time, it was on the wall staring at him. One of the sisters grabbed him fast enough to prevent his

running out of the house into the night. She locked him in her strong arms against her bosom, almost to the point of suffocation, and softly consoled him that the snake was not there. He was only hallucinating.

Still crying with fear, the boy dozed in her now tender and relaxed arms and slept. She slowly put him down on his reed mat bed. The same nightmare and hallucination, an extension of a dream of the snake, happened many times during the night. Finally, by the third day, the boy was all right and returned to sleep with the other boys in their hut.

This legend illustrates that digging mice is a thrilling, but sometimes outright dangerous adventure. A year after this incident, the boy resumed digging mice but this time he had nothing to do with trying to catch it at the escape hole. And he never smoked dagga again. In spite of what happened, mbeba are still one of the many reasons why the Tumbuka people have never thought of the dry season as being a time of drought, full of misery and suffering. The tribe, and the boy, have always thought of it as being one of the best times of the year.

ABOVE: African figurines are sometimes carved to look menacing, as they are meant to capture terrifying supernatural forces. This female figurine with large, strong arms and a child may have been used to ward off evil spirits that were threatening the woman's fertility.

RIGHT: Traditional African societies have separate huts for girls and boys. These boys are shown leaving their hut for a ceremony among the Sumburu people of Kenya.

CONTEMPORARY
LEGENDS

Since the effective introduction of European colonialism in the early 1900s, contemporary African legends have hardly been documented on a large scale. As compared to ancient legends, these contemporary legends are a product of many unprecedented social forces impacting Africa. Two interrelated factors stand out.

First, European colonialism in Africa introduced wage labor, new economic and political systems, urbanization, and Western consumption patterns. African peoples are rich with legends of how Africans adapted to, accommodated, or, in many cases, resisted these influences. A specific example is that European colonizers often imposed hut or

poll taxes on able-bodied male heads of village households. These taxes were introduced in virtually all colonial countries in Africa. This was to force otherwise self-sufficient African men to go and seek wage-earning employment on European commercial farms, in mines, in road and railway construction, and in manufacturing industries. This often involved walking hundreds, and in some cases, thousands, of miles to European commercial centers. Some of the money earned could then be used to pay taxes. These taxes were collected by European political administrators known in British colonial Northern Rhodesia, now the independent country of Zambia, as district governors.

How did Africans adapt and react to the conflicts and demands imposed by new consumption habits, which involved the acquisition of such new commodities as transis-

European colonization and urbanization brought together many Africans from different tribes. This created a fertile ground for contemporary legends. Here, men are reporting for work at a mine in South Africa.

Money that Africans earn from cash crops or wages is used to buy modern consumer goods. Here, a farmer receives money from the sale of his cotton and maize cash crops at a Ngwezi settlement in Zambia.

tor radios, money, sugar, tea, bread, clothes, bicycles, and blankets? The folk story "The Mysterious Bird" (see page 34) perhaps best depicts some of the consequences of the temptations introduced by these new consumer values.

Second, the introduction of modern commerce, industrialization, and urbanization by European colonialism brought together Africans from many different tribes. New legends emerged when Africans from different regions and tribes encountered each other for the first time in newly established urban centers of commerce, commercial farming, manufacturing, mining, religion, and education. In Southern Africa, for example, Africans from as far north as Northern Malawi; Eastern, Western (formerly Barotse Protectorate), and Northwestern Provinces of Zambia; and Mozambique all migrated to the South African gold mines. Legends abound about the experiences of the African labor migrants and members of the families they left behind.

In the Tumbuka tribe of Eastern Zambia, many young men walked single file for months through wild bush and dangerous terrain to Salisbury, Wankie, and Bulawayo in Zimbabwe (formerly British Southern Rho-

desia), as well as to the gold mines of South Africa, in search of jobs. The men initially carried all the corn mealie-meal they could on their heads and stopped on the way to cook and eat. During the early part of their long journeys, they saved their food as they were passing friendly tribes or villages in familiar territory. Eventually they walked through unfamiliar and sometimes hostile lands. They braved wild animals, spent nights in trees, and resumed walking at the crack of dawn every day. By this time they would have run out of their own food. They depended on the generosity of total strangers in the numerous villages they passed. They also subsisted for days on end on small game and wild fruit.

According to one legend, a group of men on this long arduous journey were given dry maize food from some villages. Instead of wasting the day by stopping, sitting down to light a fire, and roasting the maize, the men decided to roll a bunch of dry grass together, make it into a torch, and use it to cook the maize in the *jonjo* (frying pan) they carried. One man walking in front carried the lit dry grass over his shoulder while the man walking behind him roasted the maize in the pan. When the roasting was complete, the men ate the maize as they continued to walk briskly through the bush. Eventually these demanding journeys became less common when roads and railway lines were opened in the late 1920s and early 1930s.

Some African men who chose not to leave the village resisted the colonial hut tax in a very indirect way. With the collusion of village chiefs and others, these men were always mentally normal until news spread around that the district governor was making his annual tour to collect hut taxes. According to some Tumbuka informants, these men suddenly feigned mental illness and incomprehension of the demands of the *Bwana* (boss) for the *msonkho*, or tax. A man at one village had apparently perfected the scam so well that when the district governor called his name to step forward and pay, he responded in gibberish that even the translator could not understand. When he stood up, he feigned nervousness and confusion. His torn rags of trousers fell from his waist to around his ankles on the ground, upon which the entire village and the chief roared with laughter and amusement. He attempted to put on his trousers twice, but each time they fell off. The third time, the white man impatiently waved him off as "mentally incompetent." This is how this particular man is said to have earned his exemption and ultimately his freedom from taxes every year.

Once the young men had braved the long journey and migrated to the urban areas, so-cial voids were left in their villages. Some men returned after a year, but often many men stayed away from their villages for as long as five, ten, or twenty years. They sometimes only wrote an occasional letter or sent some money to wives and relatives. A few never returned to the village. What was a young woman to do who had just been married and perhaps had one child, and her young husband was gone for five to ten years? Among many peoples of the Eastern Province of Zambia, there is a legend that explains how many of these absent young men found a solution to their and their wives' dilemmas in a magical basket. This basket is known as a *luhengo*, *luchero*, *lubango*, or *kaselo* among groups in Eastern Zambia. It is a round, tray-like structure made from dried reeds that is

Living as hunters and gatherers meant being able to make fire. Men of the San (Bushmen) of the Kalahari Desert start a fire by rubbing two sticks together. Change among the San has been so dramatic that while twenty years ago they may have been photographed naked, today they wear Western-style clothing.

Known by many names, the *luchero* is a round basket that women use for processing food in traditional Zambia. The myth in Eastern Zambia is that some early migrants from the village returned to the village to visit their wives by flying in these baskets at night.

very important in a rural African household. Women commonly use it for carrying and processing grains, peanuts, and other foods.

This basket is believed to have been used by young men working in Zimbabwe and South Africa. At night these young men sat in the special round baskets and, using magic, flew for thousands of miles to visit their wives. At dawn, they would return in time to go to work in the mines and manufacturing industries. It is believed that this is how some of the men conceived their children in spite of their long absences from their wives and villages.

How did Africans react and adjust to the impact of urbanization and Westernization? African literature from the 1950s and 1960s depicts the many varied individual responses. The African literary classic *Things Fall Apart*, by the eminent African author Chinua Achebe, describes dramatic incidents when Christianity and Western ideas encountered the traditional African culture of the Igbo people of Nigeria. For example, when Christian missionaries first tried to convert the peoples of the villages of Mbata and Umuofia, conflicts developed and many missionaries were killed. When missionaries riding bicycles were sometimes killed, the Africans, not knowing what the bicycle would do, tied it to a tree.

Achebe writes, "Stories about these strange men had grown since one of them had been killed in Abame and his iron horse tied to the sacred silk-cotton tree. And so everybody came to see the white man."

African men and women exposed to Western urban lifestyles for the first time had legendary reactions. Some men embraced the new ideas and began to despise African culture and their "village" wives, which caused

some African women to wear miniskirts and lipstick, and to try to look like white women. These reactions were best depicted in a humorous weekly half-hourly radio play known as *Tambwali* (which means "lazy person" in the ChiChewa or ChiNyanja language of Eastern Africa) on the Zambia National Broadcasting Services in the mid-1960s, soon after Zambia's independence. This show portrayed an African man and woman as they adjusted to urban life. The play may have fueled a popular Zambian urban legend. An African woman joined her husband in the city. Before he left for work, he instructed her to "feed" (rewind) the clock at least once at noon. She interpreted the instruction literally and at noon proceeded to take food from the kitchen pot and stuff it into the back of the clock.

In his book *Song of Lawino*, Okot p'Bitek, in his unique African poetic style, perhaps

Women's daily chores in traditional society included the grinding of grains using smooth stone. Here, a young girl grinds grain in a village in Uganda. Modern urbanization forced many African women and men to adapt to new lifestyles.

best describes what African women and men may have experienced during this period of urbanization and dramatic social change in African society:

> My husband says
> He rejects me
>
> Because I do not appreciate
> White men's foods,
> And that I do not know
> How to hold
> The spoon and the fork
>
> He is angry with me
> Because I do not know
> How to cook

In the Zambian urban culture of the 1960s, similar legends were common. One song by the famous Zambian singer Alick Nkhata, titled "Icupo" (the ChiBemba Northern Zambian word for "marriage"), depicts a man in the copper belt complaining about his wife from the village who has embarrassed him before his friends. (The copper belt is located in the Northwest region of Zambia where copper mining is the dominant industry.) Unfamiliar with modern Western cuisine,

she wrongly poured *nthwilo* instead of sugar and milk into the teapot. (*Nthwilo*, a powder made from raw peanuts, is commonly added to green vegetables in traditional Zambian cuisine.) Ashamed of his wife's mistake and unmoved by her pleas, the man left his wife after only six months of marriage.

Africans who migrated to urban areas sometimes stayed for a long time with virtually no communication with members of their kinship at home in the village. Among the peoples of the Eastern Province of Zambia, there is a strong tradition for whole villages to relocate to a new site every fifteen to twenty years. The contemporary Zambian singer Nashil Pitchen composed the hit single "Aphiri Anabwera" ("Mister Phiri Came Back") in the 1970s about a young man who became a *machona* (a word used in Eastern and Northern Zambia to describe one who leaves the village to settle permanently in the city). He succumbed to temptation and the consumer culture of the urban social environment. He never communicated with his relatives. When he finally decided to return to the

Many African men who left their families to work in the towns left a void in the village as wives and members of the extended family coped without the men. This family shares a meal in a village on Lake Volta in Ghana.

Africans walked or traveled by bus or train to go to or from wage employment in the city. A famous Zambian song from the 1950s among the Nsenga people of the Petauke district in Eastern Zambia is about a man's strong desire to travel to the city to see the train before he dies. Many Zambians and Malawians traveled as far as Johannesburg and Cape Town in search of work.

village, his parents' home did not exist anymore, as they had died and the house had been destroyed according to custom. Most of his relatives were dead. He was a destitute and lonely man who had nowhere to go. Although the title of the song in Zambia is "Aphiri Anabwera" ("Mister Phiri Came Back"), it could easily be the "Legend of Machona Phiri." The lyrics are in the Nyanja language, which is commonly spoken in the capital city of Lusaka, the Eastern Province of Zambia, Malawi, parts of Mozambique, and by the labor migrants of cities in South Africa.

> *Aphiri anabwera kucoka kuwalale*
> (Mister Phiri came back
> from the city)
>
> *Kuwalale kuja anakhalako zaka zosawerengeka ndithu* (In the city, he lived
> for too many years to count)
>
> *Pobwera pamudzi anabwera ndi
> sutikesi* (When he returned to the
> village, he came with a suitcase)
>
> *Mukati mwa sutikesi munalibe kanthu
> shuwa* (Inside the suitcase there was
> nothing)
>
> *Pofika pamudzi banthu palibe shuwa*
> (Arriving at the village, there were
> no people anywhere)

> *Pofika pa mudzi anapeza makolo
> anamwalira* (When he arrived in the
> village, he found out his parents had
> died)
>
> *Anayang'ana pansi anayang'ana
> kumwamba* (He stared at the ground,
> and stared at the heavens)
>
> *A Phiri anaganiza*
> (Mister Phiri thought deeply)
>
> *Sono ndizayenda kuti*
> (Where will I go?)
>
> *Makoro banga wose*
> (All my parents and relatives)
>
> *Anamwalira kudala*
> (Died a long time ago)

In fact, legend has it that many of the men in Zambia who, after many years, returned to the sites where their villages had been located found only ruins of houses.

Some Africans returned to their villages with intentions of resuming traditional village life. One legend tells about a man who came back to the village with trunks full of suits, shoes, blankets, and wristwatches, and an urban lifestyle. He had saved and returned with enough money to afford to drink tea in the morning before he went to the fields to

The routine of village life involves elders commiserating about domestic animals, farming, hunting, and negotiating marriages for the young men and women. Once some Africans became used to urban life, they could never readjust to village life.

work in the afternoon. Every day when his work clothes were dirty from working in the fields, he would change into a fine suit. He could not readjust and fit into the social routine of the village, nor could he find a wife whom he liked. Eventually, however, his money ran out and the village diet of bread without tea became unbearable. He sat around and brooded for a week. One day, when everyone else had gone to the fields, he packed his suitcase, returned to the city, and never came back.

Traditional African society has many games and sports that people play for entertainment and competition. There are numerous games for young boys and girls that may involve spinning objects and throwing and catching small stones. Some of the most common games for young girls are *mboko* and

nthuma and for the boys, *sikwa*. Nthuma is a traditional African game normally played by young girls on the sand. Small nthuma (wild fruits) are put inside a circle. A player tries to throw one into the air and then, with the same hand, move each individual nthuma fruit in or out of the hole before retrieving the one tossed in the air. Sikwa is a traditional African game played by boys against one another. The game involves small cylindrical shapes made out of gourd. They are made to spin as far as ten feet (3m) on the sand or bare ground. Groups of boys compete against each other to see who can spin them the farthest or longest.

One of the most popular indigenous games is the *nsolo* stone game, which is well known and played from East to Southern Africa. Nsolo is played by passing stones from one hole in the ground to another. Variations of the game are played using seeds or stones in many parts of urban and rural Africa. In Egypt, this game is known as *mankala.*

Wrestling has always been one of the most popular competitive sports in many parts of Africa. In his novel *Things Fall Apart*, Chinua Achebe describes the wrestling exploits of the main character, Okonkwo. European influence brought soccer as a new team sport. Many Africans developed an interest in playing and watching the game. Virtually all African countries now have tales of legendary plays, games, and players since soccer's early acceptance.

Zambia has had many legendary players including Ginger Pensulo, Mizghabo Mkandawire, Protasho Makofi, Tom Musonda, Sheck Kapambwe, Zoom Ndlovu, and, more recently, "Ucar" Godfrey Chitalu, who died in Gabon, West Africa, in April 1993 in the fiery plane crash that claimed the lives of the entire Zambian national soccer team.

Discussing the development of soccer (or "football") in his book *Soccer in Zambia*, the legendary flamboyant Zambian soccer analyst and commentator Dennis Liwewe traces the history of organized soccer back to 1926, when the British occupied Northern Rhodesia, now known as Zambia. Britain had a very strong influence, and urban young men were instrumental in establishing what is today an internationally known national soccer team. As Africans settled in urban areas and began working in factories, mines, and other industries, recreation became an important part of their lives. Therefore, companies in Zambia and virtually all European colonies sponsored African soccer teams that formed leagues in the 1920s. Africans brought with them their traditional values, beliefs, and customs as they began playing this new game. These values introduced new legends about soccer. Because of the British colonial policy of segregation, also known as the color bar, there were separate leagues for Africans and Europeans. Teams from the European and African leagues, reminiscent of the Jim Crow laws of the American South, could never play against each other. This generated even more legends regarding which league or players were the best. Soon after the political independence of Zambia, racial segregation was abolished, and a single league, which became the Football Association of Zambia, was established. The first team to become multiracial was the City of Lusaka soccer club in 1963.

Africans have strong beliefs in charms, magic, and juju. They believe that besides personal ability and skill, certain magical charms, rituals, and behavior can help one achieve a

These wooden carvings show men playing the popular *nsolo*, *wari*, or *mankala* African traditional game.

RIGHT: Traditional African beliefs are such that individual *ng'anga*, or healers, diagnose the cause of a person's misfortune or illness by reading how a number of shells fall on lines drawn in the sand. They can even look into a person's future this way. When performed by a ng'anga in Eastern Zambia, this is known as *kuombeza*. Here, a soothsayer reads shells on the sand of Mali in West Africa.

BELOW: Belief in magic is very common among Africans. This is a wooden carving of a divination bowl from the Yoruba people of Nigeria.

desired objective. In American society, this would be comprable to sports players and coaches carrying a rabbit's foot for good luck, a baseball player ritualistically eating a specific food before a game, or players wearing the same socks if they are on a winning streak. Briefly alluding to the significance of the belief in charms and juju, Liwewe admits that in the early days charms were often used by the players: "They used to give charms to key players before a crucial match. But I must emphasize that there was no witchcraft at all. There were two important players on the team who were given charms to wear on the arms—the goalkeeper to prevent goals against him and the centre forward to score goals."

One of the most enduring legends concerns the soccer rivalry between the national teams of Zambia and neighboring Zaire. It is said that during the early 1950s, the Zairean national team, which included such legendary soccer players as Kalala, Kazadi, and Lobilo, always beat the Zambian national team by a wide margin. The very capable and experienced Zambian goalie frequently conceded some of the easiest goals. After many games in which this happened, the Zambian players privately asked the goalkeeper why he was conceding so many easy goals. His answer

stunned the other players: he said that the Zairean team must have had some of the most potent magic or juju because whenever a Zairean player shot on goal, he saw the ball as an oncoming speeding train, bus, or arrow, or a charging lion, buffalo, or leopard. Instinctively, the Zambian goalkeeper got out of the way. A second later he saw the ball behind him in the net as a goal he had just conceded.

It is not clear how the Zambian team and their goalkeeper ultimately solved the problem. Some people say that the goalkeeper consulted either a good Zambian or Zairean witch doctor or a *ng'anga*. (A ng'anga is a traditional healer who treats illness using an expert knowledge of roots and herbs and traditional African diseases. The person is not a witch doctor.) Others maintain that the goalkeeper dreamt of the solution after consulting the ng'anga. He was instructed that each time he saw something coming toward him, he should close his eyes, firmly stand his ground, and embrace the charging object tightly and trap it to his chest. Sure enough, the goalkeeper began blocking shots on goal after that and the Zambian national team began to win games against Zaire.

CONCLUSION

Myths and legends have always played an important function in African societies. These stories enhance and reinforce social solidarity among all tribes. However, the future status of these myths, folktales, and legends in Africa is in great danger. Three basic trends and patterns are emerging, driven by two strong forces of social change that have touched virtually all previously isolated preindustrial peoples all over the world: urbanization and modernization.

Storytelling entertains, teaches, and reaffirms the morals of the tribe. Here, a Masai storyteller sings and dances. The Masai live in the Masai Mara National Reserve in East Africa.

By Emmly Masanabo

As radios become more common in Africa, the traditional folktales, legends, and myths are told less often. This craft is from an exhibit designed around the theme of the radio in Johannesburg, South Africa.

First, African children and adults still narrate myths, folktales, and legends during the evenings in villages and rural communities. But even in rural areas, the significance of the myths as the dominant source of knowledge, wisdom, and entertainment is today challenged by modern education, radio, television, and the print media. In fact, Wendy Griswold, in her book *Cultures and Societies in a Changing World*, highlights the fact that one of the primary impacts of today's technology on community and global culture is the weakening of the oral tradition. According to her, it is hardly surprising that myths and legends will be transmitted less and less even among rural African peoples as modern influences penetrate what were, only decades ago, isolated communities. One possible mitigating factor is that there are signs that some of this change will be very gradual as some of the modern experiences are creatively incorporated, for example, into folktales (see "A Woman and the Monkey" on page 58).

Second, the widespread use of such mediums as television, print media, video, and radio among the African population already virtually precludes the use of many traditional and indigenous myths, folktales, and legends. What is more alarming is that while in America popular myths and legends are portrayed on television, in movies, and in books, this is not the case in modern Africa. Almost all popular myths, folktales, and legends in books, in movies, and on television in the urban African society are imported predominantly from the United States, especially Hollywood. This further decreases the likelihood that indigenous African myths will be recorded, transmitted, and popularized. This trend may lead to the total demise of this form of valuable African traditional culture.

Another ironic factor that may impede the transmission and preservation of the myths of Africa is that the myths and legends are likely to be seen as divisive. The young African nation-states are attempting to unite hundreds of tribal groups, which may have had different languages and customs. In order to enhance national unity, "tribalism" is often publicly denounced by national political leaders, by the popular press, and in most forms of African political discourse. Traditional myths and legends that appear to accentuate people's tribal loyalty, identity, pride, and affiliation may be seen as a threat to the building of the strong united modern African nation-state—as such, tribal myths may be downplayed. On the other hand, contemporary myths and legends that accentuate the birth of the new African nation-state may be highlighted, narrated, and perhaps recorded. Myths and legends surrounding soccer as a national sport are a good example.

Third, the future of African myths, legends, and folktales seems very bleak. The majority of African institutions and people, especially those in rural areas, may not have the resources and the means to document these forms of traditional culture. Things as inexpensive as paper and a pencil are beyond the purchasing ability of the vast majority of African peoples—let alone book printing, audio and video recording, and state-of-the-art electronic recording or archiving devices like CD-ROMs. Meanwhile, as urbanization and modernization continue to penetrate rural Africa and as people become more mobile and migratory, oral transmission of these myths will be increasingly difficult. Only massive efforts to somehow preserve the myths, folktales, and legends through documentation or other forms of recording are likely to preserve these valuable African cultural forms for the next generations of Africans.

In spite of the odds against them, a few Africans organize some form of informal "schools" to teach children in the villages. This woman is teaching children in rural Kenya. The school is far from the modern conventional classroom with a blackboard, chalk, books, pencils, and paper. In years to come, because of inadequate and dwindling financial resources, many Africans (particularly in rural areas) may have to settle for this type of school.

BIBLIOGRAPHY

Abrahams, Roger D. *African Folktales*. New York: Pantheon Books, 1983.

Bastide, R. "Africa: Magic and Symbolism," *Larousse World Mythology*. Edison, N.J.: Chartwell Books, 1965.

Bennett, Josephine. *African Music: A People's Art*. New York: Lawrence Hill & Co. Publishers, Inc., 1975.

Brewer, J. *Kalulu ndi Nyama Zinzace (Kalulu the Hare and his Brother Animals)*, trans. Mwizenge Tembo. London: Longmans, Green, and Company, 1946.

Campbell, Joseph. *The Masks of God: Creative Mythology*. New York: Penguin Books, 1968.

Doty, William G. *Mythography: The Study of Myths and Rituals*. Tuscaloosa, Ala.: The University of Alabama Press, 1986.

Eliade, Mircea. *Myth and Reality*, trans. Willard R. Trask. New York: Harper and Row, 1963.

Feldmann, Susan, ed. *African Myths and Tales*. New York: Laurel, 1970.

Gordon, April A. and Donald Gordon, eds. *Understanding Contemporary Africa*. Boulder, Col.: Lynne Rienner Publishers, 1992.

Greaves, Nick. *When Hippo Was Hairy and Other Tales from Africa*. New York: Barron's Educational Series, Inc., 1988.

Grimal, Pierre, ed. *Larousse World Mythology*. Edison, N.J.: Chartwell Books, 1965.

Kayongo-Male, Diane, and Philista Onyango. *The Sociology of the African Family*. New York: Longman, 1984.

Leach, Maria, ed. *Funk and Wagnalls Standard Dictionary of Folklore Mythology and Legend, Vol. One*. New York: Funk and Wagnalls Company, 1949.

Leeming, David Adams. *The World of Myth*. New York: Oxford University, 1990.

Liwewe, Dennis. *Soccer in Zambia*. Ndola, Zambia: Monterey Publishing Company, 1983.

Mazrui, Ali A. *The Africans: A Triple Heritage*. Boston: Little, Brown, and Company, 1986.

Mumba, Norah. *A Song in the Night: A Personal Account of Widowhood in Zambia*. Lusaka, Zambia: Multimedia Publications, 1992.

Neff, Jeffrey W. "Africa: A Geographic Preface," *Understanding Contemporary Africa*. Boulder, Col.: Lynne Rienner Publishers, 1992.

Ngulube, Naboth M.J. *Some Aspects of Growing Up in Zambia*. Lusaka, Zambia: Nalinga Consultancy/ Sol-Consult A/S Limited, 1989.

Nkhata, Alick. *Shalapo and Other Love Songs Original Zambian Hits from the 1950's*. London: RetroAfric, 1991.

Parrinder, Geoffrey. *African Mythology*. London: Paul Hamlyn, 1967.

_____. "God in African Mythology," *Myths and Symbols: Studies in Honor of Mircea Eliade*. Chicago: The University of Chicago Press, 1969.

P'Bitek, Okot. *Song of Lawino*. Nairobi, Kenya: Modern African Library, 1966.

Rohrich, Lutz. *Folktales and Reality*, trans. Peter Tokofsky. Bloomington, Ind.: Indiana University Press, 1991.

Schapera, Isaac. *Married Life in an African Tribe*. New York: Penguin Books, 1940.

Smith, Alexender McCall. *Children of Wax: African Folktales*. New York: Interlink Book, 1989.

Sills, David L., ed. *International Encyclopedia of the Social Sciences, Vol. 5*. New York: The Macmillan Company & The Free Press, 1968.

_____. *International Encyclopedia of the Social Sciences, Vol. 10*. New York: The Macmillan Company & The Free Press, 1968.

Tembo, Mwizenge S. "The Dry Season and the Art of Digging for and Eating Mbeba," *Titbits for the Curious*. Lusaka, Zambia: Multimedia Publications, 1989.

_____. "Tasty Mice: The Significance of Mice in the Diet of Zambia's Tumbuka People," *The World & I*, November 1992.

_____. "Where Chickens Sleep in Trees: The Importance of Chickens in Rural Zambia." *The World & I*, September 1991.

GLOSSARY

Bwana and Donna—Swahili nouns originally used to show respect. Bwana is equivalent to the "lady" in English and Donna to a gentleman. During British colonialism, Europeans appropriated the terms, particularly in Zambia, to refer to white men and women who were always bosses to Africans at work. Now the terms are used to refer to any person in a position of authority.

Chinkhali—a large clay pot that is used to cook foods in large quantities or to boil water for bathing.

Cimthiko—a specially made stick that women use for cooking.

Dambo—low-lying land that is often found at the source of rivers and streams. The area is wet and often has short green grass. Cows, goats, and sheep may graze here. It is also a source of drinking water for many villages in sub-Saharan Africa. Village wells are located here.

Delele—more than thirty varieties of green leaf vegetables eaten in the Eastern Province of Zambia and many parts of rural Central Africa. The vegetables have a very slippery consistency when cooked.

Jonjo—a special broken old clay pot or old tin pan needed for roasting dry corn or maize or peanuts.

Machona—someone who traveled to an urban area in search of a job, settled in the city, and only occasionally or never returned to the village.

Mangwanda—rattles tied to a dancer's feet.

Mboko—a game that children play in which one child conceals a small object, perhaps a stone, either in their hands, their pocket, or in one of the others' hands, and the opponent has to guess where the object was hidden.

Mphala—a hut where single unmarried young men and boys sleep in the village.

Msonkho—the taxes that were collected by the colonial administration in Zambia. The term is also used today to refer to taxes in the modern states.

Mukuyu—usually a short tree that spreads its thick leaves. There are many proverbs that also refer to its fruits, which often have ants inside even though the outside of the fruit looks good and ripe.

Nkhokwe—a structure found on the edge of an African village. It is used as storage for maize, peanuts, beans, and peas.

Tambwali—a lazy person.

INDEX